Bowl of Light

Anne Yarbrough

Publisher Information

Ruby Begonia Press

Copyright © 2012 Anne Yarbrough

ISBN: 1470003260
ISBN-13: 978-1470003265

For Greg

Preface

It was my great good fortune to live for four years on an island in the North Atlantic Ocean, off Nova Scotia. My husband and I had moved there almost whimsically. We had already taken retirement from our work as United Methodist pastors, and now we were ready to take a flying leap of some sort, drawn by the island's severe beauty and its remoteness. It was a journey of the soul for us both. We hoped to find there something that had eluded us in our plentiful American lives, even though we didn't know exactly what that something was.

Over the next four years we began to discover what we had been missing. Sometimes it walloped me over the head, and sometimes it came on a whisper. Even now it's hard for me to distil all that the island taught me. It had to do with the gifts of solitude and silence; with the integration of our work and our needs; and with learning to be both more independent than we had ever needed to be, and, paradoxically, more dependent. It had to do with the condition of not-knowing, and it had also to do with the unknowable. It had to do with an ever-flowing tension between humility and grace, neither of which is a particularly feel-good kind of thing when it's actually going on, really. It had to do with wonder.

My husband Greg was the intrepid one who made a regular voyage to the mainland for supplies, while I preferred to stay on the island. Sometimes I stayed there for weeks or months at a time. Other people only came to the island during part of the year. As you will soon see, those other people, both the living and the dead, were themselves our extraordinary teachers, to whom I will always be grateful.

Yet, for example, there was one winter when we did not have a single visitor for more than four months. But far from being lonely, I felt like a desert wanderer who had happened upon a glorious hidden oasis. The island's solitude was the single most replenishing experience of my life, a gift that awakened my senses and my spirit in ways I could never have imagined before. It was the solitude that allowed me to begin to recognize a certain luminosity in the world around me, a sense that every molecule was somehow infused with light. There had been glimpses of this for me in my life, but until I moved to the island I never experienced anything like it in such a sustained way. I kept getting flattened by glimpses of a wild holy beauty, day after day after day. Mostly that's what I did while I lived on that island, and mostly that's what I hope to share with you, dear reader.

I kept a blog while we lived on the island, and I have used some of those posts to make this book. The book is organized by seasons, but it isn't particularly chronological. For instance, one summer my garden was water-logged and paltry and ended prematurely; another year the weather was wonderful all summer long and the garden was too. Both gardens show up, higgledy-piggledy, in Season of Grace. So I hope you'll read each essay as its own little story, a reflection on its season, and not be too worried if they don't necessarily unfold into a larger narrative. Though, who knows? Maybe you'll recognize a larger narrative as well.

Montreal
January, 2012

Table of Contents

Season of Silence

Season of Waking Up

Season of Grace

Season of Harvest and Loss

Season of Silence

Introduction: Silent Season

Each day here gives us something deeper than the day before. The silence that surrounds us today is deeper than yesterday's, and tomorrow's may well be deeper yet. It is not only that we have no visitors and no phone calls. It is not only that bit by bit we have journeyed away from what passes for television evening news and no longer bother to pick up videos in town.

One day this week as soon as Greg came in from chopping wood the snow turned to freezing rain and glittering panes of ice slicked the back windows. Everything outside was glazed -- stones, branches, the indented prints of deer hooves in snow. Even the harbour water looked still as ice, until a northeast wind blew it away from the cove in graceful sheets.

On the Internet I found an old newspaper article about why there are so many Buddhists in Nova Scotia. I have my own half-formed ideas, something about the way the province lies out here on the very edge of North America, something about the way its every boundary is washed by salt waves, something about its interior forest, its silence.

But the article said it was because of the weather. A Tibetan teacher urged his students to move to Nova Scotia many years ago because the weather here -- so dramatic and changeable -- would keep them on their toes, awake to the forces of the world.

Each day's gifts are unexpected, as small as a spot of orange lichen on a grey rock, as quick as the midnight moon glimpsed through rushing clouds. We are learning to look for gifts that will tumble upon us all day even though we do not know what they will be. Every day, out here where nothing ever happens, we are a little bit more awake to the world than we were the day before.

Weather Report

Earlier this week the weather was quite cold, with snow blowing sideways across the windows and the first icicles of winter glittering from the roof's edge. Then it warmed up quickly. Last night the house trembled for hours beneath the wind's relentless power, until suddenly it relented and went away, to blow somewhere else I suppose. At midnight the air outside was warm, quiet, sated, pungent with seaweed. After such a storm the waters beyond the island continue to churn and curl and dash. The ocean pounds the cape on the southern tip, and pours down the eastern and western sides. Huge waves march single file down the centre of the shallow western channel. On the island's northern end, closest to the inner harbour, the currents from the east and from the west meet in fierce underwater combat. Then the air is still, but the ocean's deep rhythmic drum beats against the island, and its sound penetrates every living cell.

We rely on three weather reports, all of them conflicting. Usually one is accurate, although we will not know for sure which one until afterward. We do not blame the weather reports. The western cove on McNutt's Island is neither raw Atlantic Ocean nor protected inner harbour. The report from Environment Canada is taken from Baccaro Point, not far away down the south western coast toward Cape Sable. Baccaro Point sits exposed at the sea's edge. We have been there, and seen the fenced-in field of small shining instruments ceaselessly spinning as they measure the elements. The other two reports are for the Town of Shelburne, in the harbour's deepest pocket, not for the island.

He's giving wind, people say around here; he's giving sun; he's giving snow; he's giving rain. I do not know who he is. Maybe he is some Nova Scotian weather god, a dramatic sort, more Celtic or Acadian than stolid New Englander, who gives magician-like, with sudden feints and flourishes, with surprises up his sleeve, who keeps us on the edges of our seats, and plays to our astonishment.

Our Simple Life

Our simple life contains a great deal of complexity. A trip to the grocery store, for instance, involves a crotchety ATV, a muddy rocky road, a cranky boat, sudden winds and iffy harbour crossings. And our simple life is not particularly an easy life. It sometimes requires a kind of physical hardiness most Nova Scotians take for granted. So maybe you could call it, instead, the direct life.

Take our food. We don't grow our own coffee or tea, milk, butter, cheese or eggs (yet). We buy flour and molasses and sugar and salt and oil, pasta and rice and lentils and potatoes. But nearly everything else we have is stuff we've made or grown or collected ourselves. We have shelves of jellies and jams and applesauce and chutneys, and a freezer full of beans and peas and beets and chard and turnip greens and wild raspberries, soups made with rutabaga and turnip and squash and carrot and cabbage, borscht, zucchini casseroles, parsley and walnut pesto, carrot top pesto, zucchini bread, and our adopted pig from a farm near Truro. Two kinds of winter squash sit curing on the kitchen shelf and sauerkraut sits pickling in an antique crock. Herbs from the summer garden -- thyme, mint, parsley, sage -- hang from an old oar in the breezeway.

All the vegetables come from our garden. Greg makes our granola with walnuts and dried apples from our trees. We eat chanterelle mushrooms we've gathered from the forest, mussels harvested from rocks in the cove, lobsters dropped off by kind lobstermen on their way home from the sea, and haddock provided in the same way. We drink our own cider. We bake our own bread. None of this is particularly easy -- except the lobster, which just falls into our laps. But it isn't difficult, either, except for a few one-time efforts like creating the garden. It's direct, though, and so it feels more integrated, more whole, and in that sense, maybe, more simple. It's amazing to eat carrots you've grown from a package of seeds, incredible that a few sugar snap seeds can produce the profusion of peas we will enjoy all winter long, astonishing to have pancakes made with raspberries we picked near the old cellar last August, drizzled with maple syrup a friend made, unbelievable how many steps are involved in getting walnuts. And so our meals are an experience of gratitude and delight, naturally.

This is all something our own grandparents would have taken for granted. Of course you grow a garden, or at least you know how. Of course you know who raised your pig and caught your fish. But in just one generation Greg and I had lost it. Instead, for most of our adult lives we played our bit parts in the elaborate differentiation of expertises and labours that comprised the late twentieth century American urban economy. We earned money by doing certain kinds of things for which we were specifically trained, and then we paid other specifically trained people to provide us with, say, food.

And now -- through a combination of luck, foolishness and choice -- we are learning those old skills, and that attitude that most people in the world have had since time began and we only recently forgot, and more than anything else this simple life feels like some kind of coming home.

The Forest

Except for the harbour that lies below our house to the west, the forest surrounds us. It does not crowd against us anymore, though it did when we first came here. Now you can see east -- past the back orchard and the vegetable garden -- to the empty lower road. You can see the far stone wall to the south, where Greg cleared the trees last summer. But beyond these boundaries the island is a pointed vertical dark forest of spruce, and the ground beneath the forest is moss-covered bog and boulders, cross-hatched with fallen trees and branches and scrubby undergrowth.

The forest is the island's default position, and everywhere it is not something else -- our newly cleared places, an old field, a ruin, a summer camp, a road, a rocky shoreline -- it is forest.

Ten feet inside, you are clambering over dead logs that give to the touch, or treacherously collapse when you are half way over. Your feet get caught in mucky bog that emerges and disappears without warning, layered with twists of wicked dead branches, ingenious traps for trespassers.

The only paths are those made by the sheep and the deer and the ATVs. The paths of sheep and deer are narrow, and you must rely on what they had in mind when you travel there. They may not go where you think. The ATV paths are easier to follow, with their secret signals of a hanging buoy or a beer bottle stuck over the end of a branch. They lead to deer blinds deep within the forest: gnomish huts and tree houses, empty eleven and a half months each year. You stare, then retrace your steps.

Twenty feet inside the woods, and when you look back you don't know where you are anymore. There are no landmarks to give you a sense of orientation or direction. Look back toward the main road you so foolishly left. It has disappeared. On its other side, the same forest blends into the one you are standing in, so there's no perspective, really, to grab hold of. Still, there are wonders to behold: silently trickling streams that eddy into tiny rock-edged pools, deep and mysterious, where nobody ever goes. The gothic verticality of thousands of narrow spruce spires, delicately draped with an airy gray-green lichen called Old Man's Beard. The weak winter light filtering through the forest. The silence.

Once, last summer, Greg and I unaccountably wandered apart, each going in slightly different directions a few yards off the main road. I felt an alluring pull that drew me deeper and deeper into the forest. It was irresistible, an ancient druidical enchantment. I walked further and further, until suddenly my boot sank down a good foot into a bog, followed by my other boot. I was being sucked into the bog, forcefully. I was only able to fall forward flat on my face and from that position slowly extricate my feet, then reach in to pull out my boots, then crawl backward until I returned to solid ground.

I laughed while I was lying there spread out flat against the bog, deep in the forest, beyond hearing or seeing. I laughed at first with surprise, but then with an inexplicable joy. I could have lain there, filled with such gladness, forever. I think the forest is somehow dangerous that way.

The forest is the stuff of fairy tales, of being lost and finding your way again. Strange things can happen there, just beyond the known world of stone walls and vegetable gardens and apple trees, and beyond the great wood pile that Greg has made by going into the forest day after day and felling the trees, and cutting them into logs, and splitting them, so that we can be cozy and warm all winter.

Winter Solstice

Soon will come the moment when the earth, like a spinning top, leans as far away from the sun as it can. But then, in that deepest of darkness, the world will begin again to wobble toward the light. It will be nothing but the tiniest of shifts. We won't be able to observe its effects right away, except for an incremental lengthening of the days, each one by a minute or two. But already, at the very beginning of winter, the subtle mechanics of spring will have been laid down.

When we lived in the city the solstice passed without our notice. Light was everywhere, not just at home, but on the streets and in the buildings, and the lights of Christmas added color and sparkle to the ordinary nightly light — houses and streets and trees and shop windows glowing. But here we feel it when the light begins to fade at mid-afternoon. At night we look out the windows into a darkness broken only by scattered lights of solitary houses across the harbour, and the red gleam of a cell tower out on Route 103. When a late lobster boat comes in from the ocean, heading toward Gunning Cove, its strong floodlight cuts across the darkness, and we watch it go by.

There were old kerosene lamps all over the house when we first arrived, the only source of light in those pre-electricity days. There were dozens of them, hanging on the walls and sitting on doilies on the tables and on top of the old pump organ. We cleaned up the best of them and ordered paraffin-based lamp oil from the hardware store, not wanting the soot and smell of kerosene.

Oil lamps come with intricate parts, but I have had a wonderful guide to them. When Greg was a little boy he collected old ones, and ordered necessary replacement parts from Old Sturbridge Village, one of his favourite boyhood haunts. He grew up in Northern California among the moderns but both sides of his family were New Englanders, and his heart was in another age, even then. So I have been in excellent hands when it comes to learning about the clever internal mechanism for drawing up the wick.

We have electric lamps now, thanks to the mysterious conversion of wind and sun into energy. But oil lamps have provided light to this old house since it was built. So taking care of them has become a part of our lives, like chopping wood or baking bread or washing dishes or hanging clothes on the line. We are grateful that the oil lamps are not essential. Living here through the winter without electricity must have been one urgent chore after another, and uncomfortable, too. But they are a connection with the past, and they are beautiful. And so this first winter evening, as darkness falls, we will set the oil lamps aglow, and remember that we are wobbling toward light.

Wild Things

Today is a wild day, after a wild night. The house is shaking from stem to stern as the wind forces her way through all the cracks and crevices. You don't want a house to be so sealed up by insulation that it can't breathe, the experts say. That's really not a problem for us. Our house breathes fine. And today it is gasping with all the excitement, inspired by the wildness that's swirling around it. The oak tree that Burnes Goulden planted for his mother seventy years ago, when he was just a lad, and which is now too big to be so close to the house, is waving its long thick branches right in our faces as we stare out the windows. The boat is dipping and leaping enthusiastically at the dock, straining its lines in the frothing crashing waves. Every island thing wants to go wild and break free and have a wild rumpus!

Yesterday in the midst of cold, strong winds we heard a pounding at the side door and opened it to greet Arnold d'Eon, who used to own the island's sheep. He finally sold the flock to Leroy d'Entremont, and yesterday they both came up from Pubnico in an open skiff filled with eager rams. Somehow it worked out that Leroy was out dropping off rams in the raw weather while Arnold was having tea and warming up in our house. Three or four rams are on the island now, fresh from several months of lock-up on one of the ram islands south of here. They've got quite the task: eighty or ninety ewes to impregnate a.s.a.p.

The shepherds bring on the rams at this particular time to insure that the lambs will not be born at random times, when it might be too harsh for them to survive. Leroy and Arnold will take the rams off again next fall, back to the mythical ram island, an all-male world where they eat all the potato chips they want and watch football twenty four hours a day. "So," Arnold says, "today's the 21st. So five months minus five days -- May 16th, look for the first lambs."

Today the winds howl and the house shakes and the trees dance and the boat lunges and the waves crash and the clouds race across the sky and the sheep are having wild sex. It's a home-grown island Saturnalia. We ourselves are happy to be inside, baking cookies, keeping close to the woodstove.

Sunset Cruise

We returned from the mainland today in a tranquil sunset, loaded up with groceries, propane, gasoline and sharpened chain saw blades. The herring gulls put on quite a show as we crossed, circling the boat, hoping we were lobstermen about to throw old bait overboard, swooping and diving and then coming to settle innocently on the surface of the waves, puffing out their feathers.

The gulls are here all year, so we take their presence for granted. They do not elicit the thrill of a first sighting in spring or the vague melancholy that comes in October when we realize that a migratory bird has flown away. A kind of silence settles gradually over the island. But the gulls remain.

And so in winter we see them differently. Sometimes we stop what we're doing to watch them float above the spruce trees near the shore. And this evening they drifted over the harbour against a high pale blue Nova Scotia sky, lit by a golden sunset so that they themselves seemed touched by gold, as luminous as Renaissance angels.

Winter Garden

The local gardening columnist, Carla Allen, wrote recently in *The Shelburne County Coast Guard* about the power of seaweed applied to garden soil. Winter is seaweed-scavenging time, she wrote, since the late fall storms rip the seaweed from its beds and cast it upon the shore. It's there for the taking. She encouraged southwest Nova Scotia gardeners to go out there and get it, and to apply it directly to the garden, now. It will break down by planting time, she promised, and make your soil very happy.

On McNutt's Island the seaweed is mainly harvested by the wild sheep. They spend most of winter eating kelp out along the island's rocky shores. That's what they live on until the new growth of spring broadens their menu options. But there is enough seaweed to go around. So today I took Carla's advice and went harvesting, down at the cove. I covered about half the vegetable beds with several inches of rich dark seaweed, and tomorrow, if the weather stays so nice, I will finish the task. This winter gift from the sea will provide good things to our island garden soil.

Skeleton Forest

"McNutt's Island used to be so beautiful," a friend told me today. I was startled. I feel so enveloped by beauty here that at first I could not think what he was talking about. Then I realized that he meant the dead spruce trees. They are everywhere. Along the island's western side there are huge swaths blown over by the fierce storms that hit the island several times a year. A huge winter storm did the most damage, several years ago, and since then the remaining trees have been more vulnerable. Dead trees sprawl along the roads, their branches broken off at crazy angles. They teeter threateningly above the paths, only half-fallen, sharp branches pointed at your eyes, dripping with Old Man's Beard. You pass beneath them, quaveringly.

Compared to deciduous trees, spruce trees grow up quickly and begin to die quickly. And they have a shallow root system. There's not much that holds them to the earth. So they become like dominoes -- one falls into the next, and together they take down a few more. Add to their speeded-up life cycle the strong winds that rake the island, and you have the conditions we see all around us.

Just beyond our northern stone wall there is a wide swath of devastation that extends from the shore all the way to the lower road. It is a skeleton forest of trees driven mad -- indeed driven to death -- by gale force winds. Trunks white as bones lean against each other, starkly angled, austere. The ground is an impenetrable mass of rotting trunks and branches.

I understand what our friend was telling me. When we first moved here I thought the dead forests were ugly, too. But I don't anymore. His comment helped me realize how greatly my own perspective has changed during the year and a half that we have lived on the island.

Now I see the dead forests as an aspect of the island in its cycle of growth and decay. Out of the destruction something new emerges. Tiny spruce trees, no bigger than your hand, are everywhere. When you look closely you find a subtle world of mushrooms and fungi and lichen and moss colonizing the dead wood -- a world of colour even now in the dead of winter.

McNutt's Island really is, at heart, a wild place. Storms blow, and patches of forest fall, and the island is always in the process of dying and being born. It's quite beautiful, on its own terms.

It's New Year's Eve and silence has fallen on the island. Our friends have returned to the mainland. All day the lobster boats were back and forth in the harbour on calm waters, bringing in their traps before the big blizzard that will hit Nova Scotia tonight. Tomorrow morning we'll wake up to an island transformed by snow, and everything will be new again.

What's for Dinner?

Before hunting season last fall, Mark and Sid and Sid's son ("Sid's young fella," as they call men's sons around here) came by to ask whether it was okay if they hunted in the old pasture. It's an odd ten acres -- mostly forest, of course -- on the other side of the island. Somehow it belongs to us. It isn't exactly accessible, and once you get there all you can see is an old pasture being rapidly devoured by young spruce trees, even as you watch. One old timer told us it was where the community-owned ox was kept when nobody needed him, back in the day.

But Mark and Sid told us that the old pasture was part of the route the deer use to go back and forth from one side of the island to the other. If they could sit up there they would be likely to get a deer. Sure, we told them.

We love watching the deer in every season of the year. We admire their beauty and their nimble ways. I had no idea until I saw it that a deer would actually stand up on his hind legs to reach an apple on a tree. It's a joy to see a small group grazing peacefully near the stone walls or bounding through the bog on a summer evening. It's less of a joy to repair the deer fence around the vegetable garden after they have run through it, but I don't mind. The deer have been here much longer than we have. Their presence makes the island more of a magical place.

But we appreciate the hunters, too, and their long relationship with the island's deer. We observe their time-consuming preparations in October, as they repair the deer blinds and get everything ready. And we admire their successes in November.

Last week messengers carrying a huge box of frozen deer meat pounded on the door. After they left we opened the box and put everything away in the freezer: roasts, chops, and steaks, maybe twenty pounds of island venison. The hunters had been more than generous to us.

Tonight Greg is making venison roast. He'll make slits in the roast and insert garlic slivers. He'll rub on olive oil and pat on herbs from our garden, thyme and oregano that have been drying on the old oar in the breezeway. He's also making baked buttercup squash with walnut maple stuffing. I grew the buttercup squash in the garden last summer, and it's been sitting on a shelf in the kitchen. Cliff and Ardith made the maple syrup, and I harvested the walnuts.

We'll have Swiss chard, also from last summer's garden, sautéed with garlic and ginger. And, of course, our apple cider.

How we eat now is a world away from how I've eaten all my life before coming to the island. It's a revelation to be so intimately aware of the meal on the table. Today I'm especially grateful to both the island's deer and the hunters, not to mention the cook.

It's All about Wood!

It was about this time during our first winter on the island that we read the journal kept by Elizabeth Hyde, who lived here before we did. Mostly she lived here in the summers, but in the winter of 1984/1985 she stayed over, and wrote about her experience. Elizabeth was here by herself for most of the winter, and the house had no electricity or running water then. Many of her journal entries were focused on the basic tasks of survival. A friend of hers, Anne Barclay Priest, read Elizabeth's journal at about the same time we did. Her comment to us was: "It's all about wood!"

It's true for us too, even though we have it plenty easier than Elizabeth did. The house is still heated with wood, though our Pacific Energy stove is much more efficient than the old cast iron number Elizabeth used. Greg spends most of his outdoors time felling trees, cutting logs, carting them to the wood pile and splitting them. He's working on next winter's wood, a good sign of our progress. This time last winter we were using it as fast as it could get thrown on the wood pile. I call him The Woodcutter, as it has a nice Brothers Grimm ring to it.

My task is to resupply the log holders next to the wood stove. I do this every day. I have built up an extra supply in the breezeway in case we get a patch of wet weather. Our wood pile is protected, but not very well, with plastic sheeting that blows off in spite of the many many logs and rocks I have piled on top.

Before Elizabeth bought the house, the back wing (an old building that had been attached to the house at some point) was a woodshed. In those days you could walk from the kitchen into the woodshed without going outside, and your wood was always dry. The Old Fellers -- Elizabeth's collective name for the people who lived here in the past --had their priorities straight. Elizabeth turned the shed into what she laughingly called the guest wing, and we followed her direction. We put the plumbing over there, and made a laundry/mud room/breezeway, bathroom, closet and bedroom in that space. Some days I think we ought to turn it back into a woodshed, though.

Autographed House

William Acker Perry's signature is etched in the kitchen window. It is his autograph, written with elegant loops and swirls. He was proud of the house he had made, I think, and so like an artist he signed it.

William's parents, Jonathan and Martha Hagar Perry, married in 1834 and settled on the island soon after that. William was born here in 1837, the second of their nine children. You can still see the stone cellar of the first house the Perrys lived in, below the lower orchard, and the traces of their first stone walls. For some thirty years they raised their family there, and after Martha died Jonathan remarried and lived another twenty years in the old house. After his death one of his married daughters kept on living there until she and her husband moved away to Boston around 1900.

William and his brothers and sisters were island born and grew up along this shore. By then the main road and the lower road had been cut out of the forest, and fields cleared, and the lighthouse built. Other families had settled on the cove and along the southern shore between the cove and the lighthouse. There were pastures and gardens and orchards, stone walls and wells, pigs and chickens and oxen and cows, flocks of sheep, short cuts and paths, neighbours and neighbourly ways, and always the sea.

William became a fisherman like his father, and together, I think, they built this house when he was a young man, before he married Abigail Bower. William and Abigail lived together in the new house -- so promising a beginning -- for only three years, when she died. They had no children.

A few years later William married Ann Maria Allen from Lockeport. They had five children in this house, all girls. Florence Abigail was the oldest, born the year after her parents married, and Annie Maria three years after that. Both girls married fishermen, like their father and their grandfather, and they both married young, at seventeen and eighteen. They both had island weddings, most likely in this very house.

The third daughter, Bertha Eugenee, was born when the older two were five and three. They would have made a happy trio of girls to greet their father when he came home from the sea. Bertha Eugenee died when she was nineteen months old, of scarlet fever that swept the area that month. Helen Catherine came next, less than a year after Bertha Eugenee died. So then there were three daughters again, and a wash of sadness.

The fifth Perry daughter, Augusta Jane, was younger by sixteen years than Helen. Helen Catherine and Augusta Jane were spinsters. Maybe they continued to live with their parents and take care of them. It's an odd symmetry: the first two daughters married young and blossoming into family life, the middle daughter dying, the youngest two living into great old age unmarried.

When his wife Ann Maria was dying in 1911, William sold the house to James and Bertha Goulden and moved across the harbour. William -- island born and bred -- -- lived in Churchover for another six years, gazing over the water at McNutt's. He was eighty when he died. The couple is buried at St. Paul's United Church in Carleton Village, just across the harbour, with all their daughters.

For most of the nineteenth century and into the twentieth -- for the better part of a century -- this house and the house below the orchard were anchors of a sort, the scene of births and deaths and courtships and weddings and wakes. Three or four generations of ordinary island life went on here in that quiet daily way that we rarely pay any attention to until afterward.

The autographed house held so many daughters then, though they have left no such certain mark that I have found. Sometimes at twilight I think I see young girls' dreams floating along the rafters and collecting in ceiling corners, but maybe they are only cobwebs.

January Light

The day dawns cold, in a pale wash of high sky with undertones of pink. The island is glass covered: a layer of ice that shatters beneath your step. The whole island, seen from a distance today, would look like a zillion carat diamond displayed on the Tiffany blue velvet of the harbour's water.

I take a short trip down to the shore to get some sea water for the lobsters who have dropped in unexpectedly for dinner. They should have a happy afternoon, swimming around in our old lobster pot, not knowing it's a lobster pot, thinking instead, perhaps, that it's a very small sea.

But at the water's edge a deep winter silence settles around me. There are no waves today, but the tide ebbs and flows in quiet currents over the rocks. The water is so clear that I can see the bottom of the cove here, as it declines from the shore, at first in inches, and gradually out to a depth of a foot or so before it's lost in darkness. Gold ribbons of refracted sunlight illuminate an underwater world growing on submerged rocks. Forests of seaweed loom over limpet villages and moss meadows, all haloed with the rhythmic touch of streaming light. The cove is so quiet that I hear a susurration of ebbing water as it streams through the seaweed, like a long, slow breathing, like a song.

Small air balloons in the seaweed buoy its tendrils on the surface and allow it to float effortlessly in the sunlight. So it remains securely anchored to the rocks below yet fans out above to receive sun's warm blessing. Its underwater tangle of gently waving branches harbours a myriad of tiny hidden creatures: egg sacs and miniscule baby lobsters, fish larvae, periwinkles. Maybe it's their singing I hear on the ebb tide.

In the cove a loon surfaces, floats, calls, then dives. He swims beneath the surface, searching for his dinner, inhabitant of a mysterious world I can only glimpse. If I were to journey out along the length of the dock I could see the underwater cove more deeply, but instead I'm rooted here, standing on a rock, watching and listening for all I'm worth, held fast as heaven touches the sea, this shallow angle as much as I can take in, like all mortals who must shade their eyes in the presence of something holy.

Winter Robins

We've had a couple of dozen robins hanging around since the weekend. On Sunday they flew up into the oak tree and spread out over patches of ground where the wind had blown the snow away. They are a serious bunch in those distinguished vests of theirs, demonstrating quite a work ethic, like bankers in a better era. I almost expect to see each one wearing a tiny watch chain.

They don't seem to pay attention to time though. Even though it's well past the season to opt for someplace warmer they seem content to be here. When we saw the same thing last winter I worriedly emailed Christopher Majka at the Museum of Natural History in Halifax. He calmed me down by replying that groups of robins often stayed in Nova Scotia through the cold season. Odd as it sounds, it appears this is where they choose to be.

But I wondered what they could find to eat. I guessed they were getting insects in the trees, but surely the worms were hidden deep beneath the frozen earth. My knowledge of the world may be too dependent on children's books, since I do always think of robins pulling up worms. Being foolish and wrong-headed and filled with sympathy, I threw two cups of bird seed out on the broken winter grass. But my offering was beneath them and they ignored it.

Then today I was down at the shore at low tide. I went looking for our gaff, which had fallen off the boat a few weeks ago and which our friend Radar said he thought he had seen washed up past the fish house. I didn't find the gaff, but I did find the robins. They were browsing rocky crevices and seaweed and mud banks below the high tide line, and finding there, I guess, a return well worth their effort.

Windy Garden

I have tied long white strips of cloth, torn from an old sheet, to the top of the vegetable garden fence. Today the wind is lifting them up, giving the empty garden a certain liveliness.

It was my original intention to help the deer see the deer fence by letting the strips of cloth wave around in front of them. Last summer the deer were sometimes in too much of a hurry or feeling too exuberant to notice the fence. Which after all is nothing but an old fish net attached to spruce poles. The wind blows through that net just the way water used to flow through it. It's not a brick wall. I'm sure the deer would have noticed a brick wall. So they ran right through it several times, in one side and out the other, never even stopping to sample the turnips or peas.

I would come out in the morning and find an entrance hole and an exit hole, one on each side of the garden. Then I'd get the twine or whatever and mend the holes. Now the fish net has a lovely patched quality -- much better than before. Greg hung old Styrofoam buoys in front of the net. The buoys don't wiggle and wave, though. So we thought motion would help, and I tied up the strips of cloth.

We need these strips of cloth because the deer see the world very differently than we do. To us, that's our garden there, and it has a gate and a fence and please don't come in unless you are invited. To them it's the place they have always bounded through on their way from the apple orchard to the forest.

I hung up the cloth strips to remind the deer about the fence. But they have become a reminder for me, too -- about how much otherness the world holds in its large embrace. When the wind lifts them up they are like prayer flags, visible signs of a compassion that no fence can stop, that flows right on through and touches everything, everybody, everywhere.

Garden Dreams

I didn't think I would grow flowers here. The wild sheep wander around eating whatever they please, so I thought it would be a bit pointless unless I wanted to provide new taste treats for them. They ignore some flowers -- the foxgloves down in the lower apple grove, the blue flag iris along the shore, the wild roses, the spring daffodils and late summer goldenrod -- and they eat the red clover and the ox eye daisies whether I want them to or not. I thought I would just live with it. Besides, we put in a vegetable garden -- a big one -- last summer. How many gardens does one girl need?

Then Greg put a picket fence around the side of the house, with gates to keep the sheep out. (Please don't ask where the fence came from. It was of no use at all where it was before.) And, mysteriously, an entire bed of mallows sprang up within this fence, where I had dug beds the summer before but not planted anything. They stood gracefully nodding their pink and white heads all summer long. Those mallows got me thinking that I might have just the tiniest little flower garden after all.

So late in the summer I moved them around and gave them more space. Then I moved some mullein inside the fence. I love their broad fuzzy grey leaves, and the bees are so glad to cling to those yellow spires, and I thought a patch of it would look good next to the narrow walk that Greg had made with the old chimney bricks.

I dug up some yarrow and put it inside the fence, where it flourished as it never had in the field. One day a bold lamb walked through the open gate and in a few minutes had eaten all the yarrow flowers. That's how I learned that sheep like yarrow, and also that it had been doing so well inside the garden because nobody had been eating it. Come to think of it, maybe sheep like mallows, too. After that we did a better job of keeping the gate closed.

Then I sat on the wooden bench by the side door in the sun and dreamed. I would gather more island wildflowers and put them into the little garden. I didn't have any money to spend at Spencer's Garden Centre in Shelburne, much as I love wandering around there. So making a garden of local wildflowers fit our frugal life. And I wanted to collect them into one place where we could see them every day. That clump of white foxglove down in the lower orchard was a gorgeous sight, but we hardly ever noticed it in our comings and goings. And I wanted flowers that were already at home.

So in late fall I transplanted goldenrod and foxglove and blue iris and orange day lilies and violets and asters -- whatever I could find. Some will do well inside the picket fence and some will not, I guess. It was only out of respect for Greg that I didn't include any Canadian thistle. Our opinions differ on that plant. There was magenta phlox growing in the stone cellar foundation of Benjamin McNutt's house. I climbed down in there and dug up some of it, and also collected its feathery seeds. At least I hope that's what I got. We'll find out when spring comes.

Colour of Winter

The island has put on its seasonal colours even though we are not yet into winter's depths. My eyes are slowly adjusting to a world of grey, white, brown and green. The island's pied and dappled beauty is subtle now. I have to look more closely than in easier seasons to take it in.

Grey-green lichens stipple the trees and the stone walls and the boulders. The greens of the mosses are softer shades now, tending more toward brown. Three or four kinds of ferns cover the island in summer, but now they are cinnamon against the grey stone walls.

A birch tree stands out against the constant background of dark green spruce. Its bare branches claim close attention. Today it receives the close attention of some little bird searching for insects. The chickadee -- if it is a chickadee--is grey and black and white, the colours of the tree.

Emerging boulders poke their rounded forms out of the earth, ancient creatures being slowly born. You can see them more clearly now that they are not hidden in grasses and wildflowers. They are bronze and grey in a field of white.

The sky and the sea are grey today, but that word hardly describes their variety. The sea is pewter, its waves flowing peacefully into the shore. In an hour it will be something else entirely, though I do not know what. The Nova Scotia sky is a holy thing, high and astonishing, always changing. There is no moment when it is not worth your while to look up. This must be because the sea reflects the sky, so that even on the dullest day we live in a bowl filled with light.

Evidence of Things Not Seen

"There are tracks right next to the porch," Greg pointed out the window. The snow was not fresh but we hadn't tramped around in it much. Now we could see the tracks there, and once we started looking we saw more tracks leading toward a shed, crossing the familiar tracks of the deer.

Outside we found tracks leading to the picket fence, then along the narrow space next to the house, in what is supposedly a protected wildflower garden. We saw tracks leading to a stone wall, and between a stone wall and a hollow beneath the old pear tree. Those tracks looked as if the animal had entered a den under the pear tree. I remembered that last spring we had heard eerie sounds coming from beneath the pear tree. Now I wondered whether the sounds had been from a nest of new-borns.

But new-born what? Searching the Internet for clues, we thought that these tracks were what's called "directly registered," meaning the hind feet strike on top of the front feet tracks, so that there's a single line of tracks. Only cats and foxes leave this pattern. Both live in the Tobeatic Wilderness in southwest Nova Scotia and have been seen closer to Shelburne. There have been rumours of a bobcat sighting on the island. And I did think I glimpsed a fox the first summer we were here. But after somebody told me there weren't any here, I closed my mind to the fox.

Most of the time I blithely go around assuming that what I see is all there is to see. But since I don't know what to look for I miss seeing all kinds of things. Or if I see something unusual I reject it because it doesn't fit with what I think I know. This is what I fondly think of as my rational self. The animal tracks remind me how little of the world I see, how narrow is my vision.

We knew that the deer and the sheep come by here at night and that snakes are in hibernation beneath the house. But until today I didn't realize that there are other wild animals -- unknown wild animals -- that encircle our house in the darkness, like magical dreams, while we sleep. They have been walking around the house since it was built, I think.

They are among our nearest neighbours even though we've never met. Sometimes they leave a sign that they were here, and once in a long while we notice it.

Cold Spell

On Monday we had an appointment in Liverpool. We don't make many appointments since our crossing the harbour is always dependent on the weather. But we had this one to keep. The day was calm and bright but very cold. It was fortunately a high tide when we pulled away from our ice-encrusted dock, since Greg immediately realized that he wasn't able to shift the boat's gears. We scrambled to re-attach *Chopper* to the dock before we drifted too far away into the cove. I jumped back onto the dock as Greg threw icy lines to me. Eventually we gave up the effort to thaw out the gear box and trudged home.

Since we had only been gone for a little while it didn't take too long to get the woodstove going and warm up the living room again. We turned on the propane space heater in the breezeway. We use it sparingly, since it uses up a lot of propane. But all our pipes are over there, in what is otherwise the unheated part of the house. It is cheaper to keep the pipes from freezing in the first place than to get a plumber to repair them later. During last week's cold spell, the pipes froze overnight and we were lucky to thaw them out without any breakage. We don't intend to let that happen again.

Yesterday was cold but bright, with enough wind to get the turbine going. We had lots of energy. Today it's snowing again. The weather report had called for flurries but this is not a flurry. The snow is falling gently and slowly and steadily like snow in a children's book about winter. Because the air is so cold, today's snow looks like the fine airy drifts of wool the sheep leave in the brambles as they brush by them. There is no sun or wind. We will have to conserve our energy today. Our use of electricity is very hand to mouth that way.

Yesterday we tracked animal prints up from the bog right to the front porch. Greg thinks the space beneath the porch is one of its places of refuge. You can also see the prints going away from the porch and back to the bog. I'm not completely sure it is a fox but it is surely some creature that walks the way a fox walks. I wonder if I will ever catch a glimpse of the creature itself, or only see the signs of it.

To the Lighthouse

The day was bright and still, though cold. I was surprised to see that the road to the light house was covered with snow and ice. The snow had melted away around our house and down to the western shore. But the road goes through the forest, and so things are different there.

It was hard to walk in the snow since there was a crust of ice over the top. I had to watch where I was walking and concentrate. The island was very still. Sometimes I could hear the sound of the lobster boats out in the channel or off the cape. I was the loudest thing out by far, with my din of crunching snow. Had there been any wildlife near the road it would have been well warned. Every once in a while I stopped to listen to the snow-covered silence that descended when I was not walking. Then I could hear a crow or a gull, or a small bird deeper in the forest. Deer tracks crossed the road, following their own way from one part of the forest to another. The road means nothing to them.

I looked at the signs posted along the road: No Littering, Lighthouse 4 Km, sign without words. There are secret signs, too, that indicate entrances to interior paths: an orange surveyor's ribbon tied to bush, an old red taillight. Several streams have their source to the south of the island's watershed on the east side of the road. They run beneath the road down toward the western side of the island. From the road I gazed at mossy stream banks and a moss covered forest floor, bright light filtering through the spruces.

At the side of the road in the middle of the island stands a curious tree. It is surrounded by water from multiple springs, so that it stands on a small island within an island. The tree's root system must be covered by water most of the time. This tree is a conifer, but its shape is reminiscent of a hardwood tree and it is bare of either needle or leaf. From below you can look through the branches into the sky's vast blue background. Gray-white cones adorn the branches like tiny dried roses or little jewels. There's a mysterious quality to this tree, growing in moss and isolated by gently running waters.

Along the road are forests of miniature spruce seedlings. The ice has melted around the little trees, leaving each one on its own warm island surrounded by a frozen sea. Each little spruce tree is a tiny radiant life force.

Getting to the light house was glorious: all sun and no snow there, the sea so pale and calm, the sky mirroring it, high and wide, with wispy long streaks of cloud. I sat on a boulder and watched serene-looking lobster boats, all different colours, some mere dots on the horizon, others nearby.

After the warm sun at the lighthouse, I didn't want to walk back through the cold icy forest along a road shadowed now with the gloomy light of a winter afternoon. The return journey seemed much longer than the going out, even though I only retraced my steps. My occasional slips on the ice were a reminder to pay attention and not gawk so much or slide into useless meandering of thoughts as I often do.

I read somewhere that the Nova Scotia forests are an essential part of the earth's system of oxygenation, like the rain forests of the Amazon. Walking through the island's forested interior, I imagined the spirit of the world meditating on this mossy mat, breathing gently in and out.

Winter Dance

The morning snow has turned into ice, and teeters between icy rain and rainy ice while the temperature keeps falling. The spruce trees are weighted down with wet snow. They sway in ominous slow motion, from top to bottom, to the slow-dance music of a cold north-easterly wind. They look as if they could topple over from the effort of remaining vertical, continuing to dance beneath their steadily increasing burden.

The birches wave only their branches and not their trunks. The waving branches are glazed with ice. They are gently waving now, but they could just as easily break off if their ice covering gets thicker and the wind picks up. Both the spruce and the birch are strangely beautiful, transformed by winter's gifts. The trees have *gravitas* today, and quietly dance as the sky grows dark.

Eagle Sighting

We have been watching for the bald eagles. Last year we began to see the first pair of them in mid February, though for a few days we couldn't quite believe our eyes. "Are there eagles on the island?" we demanded of anybody we could find to ask. "Maybe," they would say. "Could be." These were not satisfactory answers. I'd stare out the breezeway window for minutes on end, looking. And once, as I pored over the eagle picture in my *Birds of North America*, I thought I saw the real thing winging past, out of the corner of my eye, as if to teach me a lesson about where to look. So this year we have been ready, and waiting.

I thought I saw one earlier this week. It glided over my head while I was hanging out the clothes, but I couldn't make a definite claim to it. Yesterday, though, Greg saw it flying along the shore, heading south toward the cove, in the direction of its nest. Though it seems that it's hard to miss an eagles' nest, it being nine feet wide and all, we haven't yet found it. Maybe this year we will make a wider, more thorough search.

I do not think it coincidental that for two years in a row we have sighted the eagles in mid February. They have their patterns, and slowly we will learn them. As spectacular a creature as it is, the eagle does not call attention to its arrival. It just arrives, and it's up to us to notice it.

Sheep Island

When we first came to visit this place, we missed the truly significant aspects. Instead we focused on the house itself. Could it be restored and could we afford to restore it? We thought about those kinds of questions -- the "practical" questions people learn to ask. But we did not think at all about all those aspects we barely noticed, which would gradually emerge as the important things.

We saw the ancient apple trees and their miserable fruit but we did not imagine what they would give us. Skipper brought us to the island in his lobster boat, and we enjoyed talking to him, but we did not realize how much we would come to rely on him, and on the kindness of so many others we had not yet encountered. We had no idea what effect weather would have on us, nor living so close to an untamed world.

And then there were the sheep. There have been sheep on the island for as long as anyone can remember. When the settlers made this their home, each family had its own flock of sheep. The sheep roamed the island in larger flocks, and once a year they were gathered and shorn, and once a year they were gathered and culled. Each household had a distinctive earmark for its own sheep, so they were easily identified at shearing and culling.

As late as the 1980s the island's sheep were still owned by several people. Elizabeth Hyde owned some, and Harry Van Buskirk, the keeper of the lighthouse, and I think Anne Priest kept a few sheep here as well as on Blue Island, and Tom Perry, who owned sheep on other islands to the south of McNutt's. Later Elizabeth Hyde bought the Perry and Van Buskirk flocks. After Elizabeth's death, they were sold to Arnold d'Eon, who just this winter finally sold them to Leroy d'Entremont. Leroy continues the old pattern: he will gather and shear the flocks in summer, and gather and harvest them in October, and he will bring the rams in late December, to insure that the lambs will be born in the mild weather of late May. Other than those interventions, the flocks are on their own.

McNutt's is one of a chain of islands along Nova Scotia's southwest shore where sheep have been kept from time out of mind. In winter these sheep survive on the seaweed that washes up along the islands' rocky shores. They seem to survive quite well, and people say their foraged diet contributes to the excellent taste of the lamb.

Since we live here all year, we have the unique privilege of watching how island sheep manage in the winter. We can see them off in the distance, on the rocky point that encloses the cove, grazing away peacefully on most winter days. And sometimes they amble up the road or through the forest and arrive at the back orchard, as they did yesterday. They graze what vegetation they can find among the ice and slush, moving down to the lower orchard and then through the forest, following a familiar route. There are other flocks on the island, one at the Horseshoe and one -- the largest -- at the lighthouse. But this flock -- of about twenty or so -- is the one that grazes along the island's western side, where we live.

We do not really think they have come to visit us when they come here. We know they are always in search of food. In all seasons this old farm provides it: in spring the tender tips of pruned apple branches and the green furled shoots of fern; in summer an abundance of clover and daisies and forget-me-nots and grasses; in fall the windfall feast of apples.

When we spy the sheep we always call to each other and come to look. Their presence around the house or in the apple grove feels like a version of grace: unmerited, unexpected, uncontrolled. They happen by, nibbling the brown dead grass, keeping to their own inner compass. They leave according to their own schedule, which they do not share with us. Our interest and attention and affection for them is unreciprocated: we are not a part of their world, though they are very much a part of ours. Their complete indifference to us is an aspect of their profound otherness, which is in itself a gift. The sheep recalibrate our place in the world. We are here to watch and wonder at woolly mystery, that visits as it pleases, the way angels used to visit, but unlike angels bearing no message as far as we can tell.

Seeking Eagles

Yesterday the sun was shining and the wind was quiet and we decided to search for the eagles' nest. I had seen a photograph on the Internet of an eagles' nest on the ground and I was sure you couldn't miss it. We had an idea of where to look, in the south western part of the island, between the sheep pen and the lighthouse. So we headed down that way.

Along the way we examined numerous animal prints crossing the icy road and wondered what they might be. They were partly melted and we are not very knowledgeable yet so mostly we point and ask each other questions that neither of us can answer. We observed the rivulets streaming down the hillside, along the road, and beneath the road down to the cove. Though they are still edged with ice and snow, they are gurgling, and bright green algae strands float in their shallow currents. Just beyond the pen we surprised the flock of sheep that lives in that area. They ran away with great urgency, leaping over fallen trees and looking back at us as if we were truly a danger to them, although we only stood still and waved a friendly greeting.

We did not find the eagles' nest, but we did discover stuff abandoned or left behind or washed up on the island. We found an old golf cart missing its wheels, sheeps' rovings, ruined cellar foundations, tumbled down stone walls and piles of stones the old fellers made when they cleared fields. Washed up along the cobble shore we found battered lobster traps, useful nets and rope, and a bright red and blue plastic toy boat in excellent condition. Sometimes you undertake adventure with great noble purpose but instead find other wonders along the way.

A Sheep's Tale

Six sheep are in the back orchard today. We have to give up our theory that the sheep come around in the winter only when the tide is too high for them to eat the seaweed that has washed up along the shore. Because the tide is not at a particularly high point today. So there's more likely a simpler explanation for their visits. Maybe they are coming by more frequently now just because the snow has melted off.

One young sheep here today has a tale attached to her. She was born last May, but she missed getting her tail docked along with all the other lambs in July. Her long tail marks her as a bad flocker, or the lamb of a bad flocker. So she would have been culled last October, lest she pass on that individualistic trait. But through a small sequence of events she escaped her fate.

There's a hub-bub on culling day, because the shepherds are running all over the island trying to gather all the sheep, and the sheep are hiding in the woods or running away. One of the shepherds caught this particular long-tailed lamb and tied her to a tree along the side of the road. He intended to go back later and pick her up after he had herded another flock down to the pen.

In the meantime a couple of visitors came on the island that day. They knew nothing about the sheep gathering that was going on. They only saw a lamb tied to a tree. Not really thinking, but with the best of intentions, they untied the lamb and she scampered off into the woods. The shepherds told us about it once they discovered what had happened, and asked us to keep a look out for her. We did watch for her, and she turned up around the house later in the day. But we decided not to go back down to the pen again, so we didn't have a chance to let the shepherds know she was here. To tell the truth, our failure to act wasn't entirely innocent on our part.

Greg even named her: Cassandra. She may not have a strong flocking instinct, but every time I see her she is with the flock. We know of one lamb whose flocking instinct was so bad he was constantly wandering off or being left behind and frantically bleating to his mother. He was a basket case from May to October, day and night. We were planning to make a special effort to point him out to the shepherds on culling day.

But Cassandra is not like that. Maybe it was just bad luck that she missed the July gathering and ended up marked by her long tail. If so, then it was just good luck (for her, anyway) that those two strangers came along and untied her.

Hare Hearsay

Sometimes when I say rabbit somebody will tell me these are not really rabbits, but hares. But then I've heard people call them both names. The first one Greg and I saw was last spring, along the lower road from Mark and Patsy's camp to ours, sitting very still. The second one I saw while I was painting the picket fence early last summer. It was hopping peacefully from the back orchard stone wall to behind the tool shed, and it was followed by a quiet and slinky mink. Greg saw one in early summer, along the southern stone wall, while he was cutting brush. They could be hares, or they could be rabbits. I guess if we saw a winter hare with its white colour we would know for sure, since the cottontails don't change their colour. But we haven't.

What I am about to tell you is almost all hearsay. The story is that there used to be hares in abundance here, back in the old days. The old days go back at least as far as the 1960s and 1970s, when Harry Van Buskirk and Barry Crowell were the lighthouse keepers and their children regularly set snares over on the south eastern part of the island. Rabbit stew was an island staple back then.

Then, sometime, somebody had a mink farm somewhere on the mainland around Carleton Village or Gunning Cove, and somehow the mink got over to the island. Maybe they swam, or maybe they stowed away on a lobster boat, or maybe somebody brought them over here on purpose, since they prey on rabbits and snakes. Nobody knows, or if somebody knows nobody tells. If the mink were brought over to keep down the hare population they may have been mighty successful in their work. And if there are foxes here then that would be another serious predator.

But then we don't really know how many hares or rabbits are still on the island. Lately I have noticed tracks in the snow that I think could be one or the other. Especially in the woods between our stone wall and the old field where the hotel used to be. Like so much else, we may think they are not here, when we just haven't yet acquired the awareness or the skill to look for their presence, or to understand the signs we see.

Lull between Two Storms

The last storm began on Thursday. It was strong enough that even Greg did not venture outside much for three days. And this evening a new storm will arrive. It is even now making its way up the East Coast from below New York and over the Gulf of Maine. Then it is due to cross the province and slam into Cape Breton and New Brunswick again. This is the pattern of our winter storms.

There will be high winds -- maybe very high this time, as much as one hundred kilometres per hour tomorrow, which takes it well into gale force and almost to hurricane force -- snow and sleet and, later, rain. This will be the tenth or eleventh severe winter storm of the season. But here on the southwest coast the storms pass over, on their way somewhere else. No matter how harsh they are to us, we usually do not get the worst of it.

This morning I awoke to the ancient sound of the woodcutter splitting wood. It's a rhythmic thump, thump, thump as the maul swings downward with all the upper body force at the woodcutter's command, slicing through the log, hitting the wide stump on which the log is vertically balanced. It is an activity I don't like to watch. A band saw once snapped in Pugwash and beheaded one of Greg's ancestors. It makes me leery of sharp objects.

Today is the lull between two storms. We have emptied the ashes and the compost and brought in enough wood for two or three days. Greg has moved *Chopper* down to Skipper's wharf in the cove, where she will lie safe from the winds. He has brought his tools inside and closed the shed doors and latched them. He has moved a full propane tank next to the tank that supplies the breezeway heater, so if it runs out he won't need to go all the way to the shed. He has secured the garbage cans so they won't fly about. By now we have experienced stronger winds than what is expected tonight. So we have some sense of what's coming.

Today is well above freezing, and the air is calm and the harbour tranquil. This morning a fine powdered snow covered a smooth crust of ice. We went looking for prints and found some lovely ones. The more we read and compare the prints we have seen with the prints in books, the more I believe we are seeing hare tracks, not foxes. You may wonder how anyone could confuse hares with foxes. It is not that hard to do if you are a beginner. A beginner doesn't know a good print from a poor one. Then, slowly, the more you look at them, the more clearly you see.

Things become less sharply edged, less fearful, less dramatic, the more you know about them. A bit of familiarity reveals fine variations, too, and makes the whole thing more interesting. The coming storm will not be so bad. "She'll be breezing up," Skipper tells us, which sounds about right. Greg is careful when he splits wood. Foxes become hares (or, maybe, rabbits). We savour this lull.

Give Us This Day Our Daily Sun or Wind

This afternoon a wild westerly wind is blowing and the sun bounces off a harbour churning with white-capped waves. It's a wide awake day, cold and lively, after a night of high wind and ice and rain. The wind holds the house in an enthusiastic embrace, pleading with it to get up and dance an unruly lumbering winter stomp to the tune of its loud brass band, a Mardi Gras of percussive bass with overtones of wail and screech, in defiant, wake-the-neighbourhood surround-sound. Let's dance! The wind is yelling over the noise of itself.

Today we have a lot of sun and a lot of wind. It's the perfect combination that gives our fancy batteries a big charge and gives us more electricity than we can use, unless we plan to spend the afternoon in a hot shower, hopping out now and then to use the vacuum cleaner and the power saw.

Our house had done without electricity for a hundred and fifty years before we installed the solar tracker and the wind turbine. It had seemed lovely to do without, but impractical. Now, hidden inside its walls, are the wires that allow us to light the rooms, use the Internet, listen to music, and keep our food cold, not to mention fire up all those power tools.

But we can't store this power. Our batteries, once filled, decline slowly but inevitably. They need constant recharging, from tonight's wind and tomorrow's sun, or any combination thereof. Even though we have more than we need, we can't save it up for a rainy windless day, and since we're not on a power grid we can't sell it to anybody. Today our energy is abundant, and tomorrow it may be nothing but a trickle.

The ancient Israelites got into trouble out there in the wilderness when they tried to store the manna that came down from the sky as unmanageably as does our electricity. They thought they were wise to collect more than they needed, engaging in the sort of industrious and resourceful behaviour the world admires. But the next morning the manna was mouldy and rancid and they had to throw it all out. They learned, eventually, gratitude for a daily sustenance, a gift of life they could not control.

Today electrical current spills through our house, a blessing that pours out of the sky like a cup running over. And we must simply live unto the day, learning the wilderness lesson whether we like it or not.

Bones

Not fifteen yards from our house, on the northern side, lies a small wild place, hidden beneath a grove of spruce: a sheep graveyard of their own devising.

One ewe's bones are an undisturbed pattern of ivory laid out on a bed of spruce needles and moss. It is as if she had simply lain down in this quiet place, and then, oh-so-slowly, over the years, been distilled to her essence. We have watched the flock seek refuge from heavy rain beneath these very trees. I love how these bones lie so near to our own waking and sleeping.

You sometimes see, in medieval painting, a *memento mori* -- a reminder of our mortality. It may be a skull or a skeleton and sometimes it even has a sign attached, like a cartoon caption, with pointing arrows: memento mori. Not too subtle. It is tucked along the edges of the painting, away from the main action. It's something you have to look for. It's not meant to be threatening or frightening. It's more a way to shift the viewer's perspective, away from the apparent reality -- the flirtations of the richly dressed courtiers and ladies who command the painting's foreground, for instance -- to something else quieter, deeper, both more consoling and more real.

The sheep graveyard is a *memento mori* for me -- a small sign, tucked away in the edges, that life in all its heartbreaking beauty does at last lie down, and death receives it. Ash Wednesday is tucked away too, hidden at the edge of things, quiet, deep, consoling, real.

Lull between Two Woodpiles

Our wood pile is in a lull. At the beginning of winter we revelled in how much wood we had, a wall of wood, split and stacked, long, high and wide, of spruce and apple and birch. We were rich in wood. But by the other day it was almost gone. I don't know how this happened so quickly. It reminded me of when you think you have plenty of money and then all of a sudden you see you don't. How did that happen, exactly, you wonder.

It's not that we don't have wood. We have a huge pile Greg has made since December, a wall of wood, split and stacked, long, high and wide. But it is the wood for next winter's heat, not for now. It must dry and age until then, when it will be ready. It will be of great use next winter. But it is of no use at all right now.

We can scrounge our way through this lull. There are plenty of standing dead trees around. Come to think of it, we are rich in standing dead trees. Greg can cut one down and chop it up and we can burn it right away, since it's pre-aged. And down by the sheep pen there's a huge pile of well-seasoned slab wood -- the remnants of Skipper's lumber milling over a year ago.

It's another lesson in living hand-to-mouth, an aspect of late winter when the wealth of harvest is running out faster and faster. Still, the temperatures are rising. Soon we'll be in and out of the house all day, too busy with spring projects to pay attention to the fire in the woodstove, which is how winter finally ends.

Stardust

We are surrounded by darkness here. There is no ambient light. Nothing mediates our experience of the sky on a moonless, cloudless night. It is beautiful, yes, stunningly so. In summer I gaze upward in awe and swear I'll learn more constellations so I can understand a bit of this overhead wildness, get my bearings and find my way around.

It's just the tiniest shift, though, from awe to terror. In winter the stars are cold glittering points, beaming messages billions of years late from a place that no longer exists. The night sky swirls and dips and lurches. Constellations swing from place to place, planets reel across the heavens, the moon rises and sets in random places along the edge of a dark looming endless bowl. The Milky Way slides across the sky from angle to angle, a loose belt in the engine of the universe. There is nothing you can count on up there, except for a cold glitter coming to you forever from before time began.

The immensity of this unmediated sky disorients and terrifies me. The stars remind me of that essential dust which is my beginning and my end. Remember you are dust, the stars sing silently. On cold starry nights I'd rather be inside.

But then it's also just the tiniest shift from terror to awe. Their cosmic song is a promise of some unimaginable goings-on beyond our ephemeral selves. The starry night will receive our dust, our molecules, our glittering motes and beams, and we shall be at once nothing at all and at one with all, as it all swirls on.

On the Edge of a Biosphere Reserve

McNutt's Island is on the edge of a UNESCO Biosphere Reserve. These reserves are protected areas not subject to human activity except for research and monitoring, and some traditional uses by local communities. The Southwest Nova Scotia Biosphere Reserve consists of the core area, made up of the vast Tobeatic Wilderness and Kejimkujik National Park. Then, like a doughnut, all the rest of southwest Nova Scotia -- five counties-- surrounds the core area and is called an area of cooperation. Since we sit out here at the edge of south-western Nova Scotia, we are on the edge of this area of cooperation.

There are about four hundred UNESCO Biosphere Reserves around the world, and thirteen in Canada. The Southwest Nova Scotia Biosphere Reserve is the first in Atlantic Canada. The reserves are places where environments are monitored and conserved, where scientific research is carried on, and where large-scale extractive processes (for instance, logging or mining) are not.

Within the Tobeatic Wilderness and Kejimkujik National Park are a wide variety of animals and plants including endangered species sited in an environment of forests, lakes, marshes, bogs, the headwaters of nine rivers, and archaeological sites important to the Mi'kmaq First Nations. You can paddle and portage through a landscape that evokes the time when these rivers were the primary routes for the Mi'kmaq travelling back and forth between the Bay of Fundy and the Atlantic coast. One of my dreams is to do some of this paddling, maybe as early as this year.

The Biosphere Reserve sits on the edge of my consciousness, something significant just out of sight. The interior of southwest Nova Scotia has a compelling wildness to it. Our first direct experience of that wildness came when we drove from New Brunswick to Shelburne almost two years ago, in late spring. Consulting our map, we turned left from the Annapolis Valley and entered the interior. Every once in a while highway signs announced, unnecessarily, "Rough Road Ahead." We were on a major secondary road, one of a few that crosses the province along the shorter north-south axis. Sometimes we encountered a few houses close together, but aside from that we encountered this astonishing emptiness.

We had turned off from the main highway without a full tank of gas, never thinking that there wouldn't be a gas station along the way. As we got closer to empty, Greg reminded me that according to our map we would soon come to the entrance to Kejimkujik National Park. "Don't worry," he said with confidence. "There will be a gas station there." We envisioned not only a gas station but also restaurants and ye olde souvenir shoppes -- a little cluster of ticky tacky. Is there any other way to enter a national park?

Apparently there is. The entrance to Kejimkujik was just that, an entrance, with no parasitical excrescences attached for the benefit of the bored or the unprepared. Woe to the one who set off without having packed a picnic lunch and filled up the gas tank! And so we Americans learned our first lesson about travelling southwest Nova Scotia style.

Since Europeans and Americans began to settle this area sporadically in the seventeenth and eighteenth centuries, the small population of south-western Nova Scotia has clustered along the coasts -- the biosphere's area of cooperation -- and left the interior alone. Over the years, the main threats to the integrity of the interior environment have been not from population growth but from mining and logging. Now its layers of wilderness, national park and biosphere reserve designations protect this vast place.

Even though we are out on the edge of the Biosphere Reserve, and don't really think about it all that much, its wildness balances the other, more immediate wildness we encounter, the sea.

Sheep on the Point

The sheep are out on the point today, forty or fifty of them, in three distinct groups. A dedicated sheep voyeur, I can watch them quite clearly from here with the binoculars. Many are lying down, close to one another, nestled on eel grass or cobblestone. Others are standing around eating the seaweed which is plentiful along that shore. They are on the leeward side and protected from the rising wind.

In their thick fleecy coats, they seem not to mind the flurrying snow, and today's just-below-freezing temperature may seem balmy compared to the often bitter cold of winter. If the wind gets too strong they will head inland, with a minimum of fuss, to seek the protection of the forest. But for now they appear tranquil, as they usually do. Very little in life seems to bother the sheep.

Yesterday the local flock of about nineteen was back around the house, nibbling away. They spent the night behind the vegetable garden. Then this morning they headed down past the fish house, returning to the point via their cove shore route.

The black faced ram is still with our local flock. Greg has named him The Major because he is the very model of a modern major general. Today he is lying down near the sea's edge, a little removed from his group, looking quite dignified. He is always dignified, and imposing. We think the girls actually run the show, but allow him to assume that he is in charge. The ewes are almost half way through their pregnancies, which commenced soon after Leroy and Arnold released The Major and his brother rams on December 21st. So we will see the new lambs around mid-May.

The ordinary behaviour of wild sheep on one of Nova Scotia's sheep islands is not observed or reported very often anymore, I think. Now their presence is so much a part of our lives here that we sometimes forget how fortunate we are to be able to watch them, and what an unusual experience it is to have these calm and woolly neighbours who manage quite well for themselves.

Season of Waking Up

Introduction: Island Music

The trilling of the toads began eleven days ago. Now every evening they sing their abundant song, a chorus that floats up from the cheerful neighbourhood watering hole that is their gathering place. There are no divas in the toad world. They are a harmonious lot, and they sing together. I imagine that if I were to tiptoe around the island at night I would hear them in every bog and swamp and low damp place: the whole island giving off a hopeful trilling sound.

In the middle of the night we hear the loon who has settled onto the cove water. Her call is singular. No living thing could resist the loon's call, and yet she is floating out there in the darkness by herself, at least for now. It is said that loons winter in the salt water and breed on the lakes in summer, but there are a few loons who spend their summers here in the cove, their lives elsewhere mysterious to us.

The wild bees are already hovering along the branches of the apple trees, even though the buds have not yet opened. If the world is quiet enough around you, you can hear the tiny sound of their wings beating against the air. I have read that the various sorts of wild bees emerge from their secret places exactly when their food supply is ready for them. I wonder how they can find what they need, since when I look around the only flowers I see that are open for business are the daffodils. On this subject, I imagine the wild bees know things I do not.

I heard the white-throated sparrow for the first time today. If there were a Church of the Wild Things -- and maybe there is; who knows? -- this would be a holiday, or, as they were called back in the day, a holy day. But then if we were to celebrate such things, every day would be a holy day and we would never get our work done. There would be First Trilling Night, and a Loon Vigil, and an uproarious Wild Bee Day. And when the white-throated sparrow returned to the island from God knows where, and perched impossibly high on a dead spruce tree and opened his beak and poured out his luminous notes for the first time, we would drop our rakes and stand in silent, gaping wonder.

How Spring Comes

Saturday was windy but filled with sun. It was warm enough that I sat outside next to the house, sheltered from the wind, and read a book Greg had ordered from the library, Bill Gaston's *The Order of Good Cheer*. I hope this book doesn't end, though I see that the library expects to get it back on March 24th. While I read I watched a single lobster boat in the harbour just beyond the point, to-ing and fro-ing over its traps.

In the mid-Atlantic, where we lived until now, spring came all in a day or two with a huge ta-da! There was no question about it. In Washington DC each year I looked for that one moment when the trees put out their new leaves, so that all at once the city (which is filled with deciduous trees) was wreathed in the palest, faintest green.

Here the trees are mostly spruce, and keep their colour. Instead of any obvious signs, it is the light that changes everything. On Saturday the sun poured over the island and turned it gold. The moss that covers the lower orchard was bronze and cream, and the rockweed waved goldenly in the cove water, and the ends of the logs in the woodpile were round and flat and yellow.

The boulders that are not grey by nature were golden, with flecks of gold, and old grey rocks wore chartreuse moss. The dried grasses along the shore and in the old fields were pale gold. Lichen on stumps and rocks were dark amber, the colour of maple syrup in sunlight. The tide pools and the mud puddles were mirrors of yellow light held up for the sky to see. Everything either absorbed the sun and became luminous, or reflected it, like the harbour did at the end of the day when the wind died down and sunset brought the whole thing to a close.

Soon more particular signs will show up. The first snake will unfurl along a rock, streams will slither and clatter down into the cove, tiny fern shoots will emerge next to the lower road. For now, though, spring is not yet anything in particular. It's just the light, everywhere.

On the Edge of the Gulf of Maine

We are just beyond the edge of the Gulf of Maine, which officially ends at Cape Sable. But something as huge as the Gulf of Maine doesn't stop at a boundary line. McNutt's Island, with its glacier-scraped rocky shores, its bogs and boulders and marshes and forests, its beds of rockweed and Irish moss, its eagles, ospreys, great blue herons and cormorants and its colony of seals, shares the habitat of that great body.

And the waters beyond the island are swayed by the powerful tides that define the region. Our friend Peter, who goes long line fishing in summer and fall, when it isn't lobster season here, says he and his crew usually don't go out during the week of the full moon. The tides can be so strong then that fishing becomes unproductive. I wonder at that. Imagine your practical, daily life affected so directly by the tides of the ocean and the phases of the moon.

The great power of the underwater ebb and flow, the churning back and forth, makes the Gulf of Maine one of the most productive marine life areas in the world. It's actually a sea, mostly enclosed by underwater banks and elevations, with a deep channel that allows the waters of the Atlantic to rush in toward the Bay of Fundy and then pour out again, so that the waters are continually renewed. There's a gyre, too, an ocean current that flows counter-clockwise and constantly stirs everything within the nutrient rich soup pot that is the gulf.

On the surface -- if you are sailing across it, say, on the ferry from Maine to Yarmouth -- the Gulf of Maine appears to be all horizontal. The view is undifferentiated waves, as far as your eye can see. Nothing is happening here, you might think to yourself. And all the while just beneath you is a submerged many-dimensioned world of mountains and plateaus and valleys, sunlit shallows and dark depths, currents swirling and rushing, and secret places not yet known.

Tide Pool Worlds

If you walk northward along the western shore from our house you soon come to Indian Point. It's a remote place where the harbour seals enjoy the sun, where we once found two rams in a state of regal retirement, and where on another early foray we came upon a fawn, curled up, looking at us, not moving a muscle.

Indian Point has fantastic tide pools. A tide pool is always in process. Each one is a small isolated world of its own, and then the high tide washes over it, and it loses its separateness and becomes at one with oceanic vastness. This week tiny fish lurked in the tide pools, like shadows. They darted into mud banks and crevices when they sensed my presence. I wonder if these little fish cling to their own pool when the high tide comes in, thinking it safe, or whether they swim bravely away into the wide sea.

Algae drifted beneath the tide pool surfaces, spring green and diaphanous. They look innocent, but they may be quietly planning their ultimate takeover of the world -- the big world, not this little one. Or they could be as graceful and lovely as they appear, giving safe harbour and food for small creatures. Or both, maybe, since they belong to this ambiguous world, where something's always washing in or washing out, being born and dying, bearing its own identity and becoming part of everything else.

Subtle Season

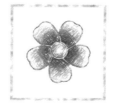

A song sparrow was hanging out near the bird feeder yesterday, looking fierce. I don't know his story. He doesn't make his winter home here, so he has come from away. But how far he has traveled, whether across the great Gulf of Maine or along the mighty St. Lawrence River, I can't say. Anyway, now he is here, hopping about below the bird feeder. He is small, and commonly regarded as common, and easily overlooked. He does not stand out, really. And yet he has just completed an astonishing feat.

Spring arrives on the island like this. The signs are subtle and at first glance nothing special. A few dark-eyed juncos arrived along with the song sparrows. I met one of them yesterday as he was sitting on a gnarly branch of the old pear tree. His beak was stuffed with the lichen called old man's beard. "Hello!" I said to him, "Welcome back!" He just looked at me, but he didn't fly off.

I wonder if I lived in a place that had a great variety of song birds whether I would take any notice of these commonplace birds. I think I would probably go for the showy types, the celebrity birds, the shiny bright ones, and not pay any attention to these. And yet they are miraculous, in a modest kind of way, and bear close watching, like this island spring itself.

Goodbye, Orion

Since I only know a few constellations, I notice when one of them disappears. A bit earlier each night now, Orion slowly slips away below the western horizon. By midnight he is gone. Just after our last frost date, in May, he will have travelled out of sight completely. Orion is a migratory constellation, cart wheeling south as the hummingbirds and monarch butterflies and songbirds are flying north. I imagine their greeting as they pass each other in the sky: birds and butterflies dipping their wings in tiny salute, Orion silently pointing their way northward.

I miss Orion already. I love the way he dances across the cold night sky. I step outside the breezeway door on a clear night and think I must be peering over the very edge of the universe. Familiar Orion helps me focus on what I can recognize in that vastness, and helps keep my primal fears in check. I think he has been doing that for people for a long, long time. We can let him go for a while, in warmer seasons, when we are naturally braver and more at ease.

Odd and topsy-turvey as it seems to me, Orion's gradual departure is a sign of spring. And he will return, this magnificent figure, next winter.

Stones Rise Up in Spring

Each spring, from deep within itself, earth pushes and pulls and groans and sighs. And each spring, slowly, spring by spring, the stones emerge.

Intense heat created the bedrock from which these stones come, back when McNutt's Island was part of Pangaea. Then North America, Europe, and Africa were all one. After Pangaea broke apart the molten bedrock cooled and hardened. Later, the Laurentian Ice Sheet slipped down from the north. Ice scoured the land, tearing up rock and slab, tossing it about to make this picturesque and deadly coastline. The ice retreated, and left behind a landscape of broken rock.

Then gradually the earth warmed. Forests returned and their growth and decay laid down soil over the stones. But beneath the soil the stones remained. The early settlers on McNutt's Island -- the Old Fellers -- pulled them from the earth and tossed them in rows to clear their new fields, and also to build these walls, our reminders of their labour.

But more stones remained beneath the earth. Each year's seasons of freeze and thaw continue to lift the stones slowly upward through the soil toward the surface. If you look closely at a stone embedded in the earth on the path to the fish house, you find a narrow dark band around the base, a newly exposed surface. There's a small gap around the stone where the ground has heaved and pulled away, making room for its passage into the light. It's a sign of spring that you can barely see, when the stones rise up.

How to Keep Warm

It has been cold here -- way, way below freezing -- for the past couple of days. This season, which for purposes of accuracy we will not actually call spring, swings back and forth between extremes. One day last week I was outside raking up dead ferns in a short-sleeved tee shirt. Today that wouldn't work out so well.

There are two basic ways for us to keep warm when it's this cold. There's the day-time way: plenty of logs in the wood stove that sits in the middle of the living room and heats this one room pretty nicely, as long as there's no cold wind blowing in from the west, through all the tiny cracks in the house.

Then there's the night-time way: piling on the blankets in our unheated bedroom over the living room. We use a combination of an old wool blanket that came with the house, two quilts, ditto, one on top of the other, and then, on top of everything else, a fat layer of cotton comforter we brought with us when we moved here. I think the layering itself has some effect, since with each successive layer you are trapping pockets of air that effectively create more insulation. Of course one decent goose-down comforter would do the trick. But we don't own one, and we do own this other assemblage, and it works.

The first summer we lived here, Anne Barclay Priest emailed us to say that she wanted to come and visit. She would come over in her outboard motor boat, she told us. Anne is the author of *Trafficking in Sheep*, her memoir of buying a summer place at Green Harbour in the early 1970s, and later buying Blue Island and becoming an owner of sheep. During that time she became a good friend of Elizabeth Hyde, who owned our place for over thirty years, and died in 1993.

Anne laid out her route for us: she would cross the mouth of Jordan Bay, then round Cape Roseway, at the southern end of McNutt's Island, enter the Western Passage, pass along The Point, and come into Hagar's Cove. It's the way she used to come when she visited Elizabeth, she told us.

On the day of our meeting we watched from the shore as Anne steered her skiff along the Western Passage and headed into the cove. She moored in the cove, untied the dinghy that trailed behind her skiff, and rowed ashore, up to the remnants of the haul-up Elizabeth had built and used long before. After she tied up, she clambered over the old haul-up and we forged our way along the over-grown path from the cove to the house. Anne was already in her eighties that summer and still a force of nature.

Before she arrived, I worried that Anne might not approve of the changes we had made. But she enjoyed the wind turbine and the solar tracker and the idea of having electricity in the old house. She admired the washing machine and the indoor plumbing and told us Elizabeth would have loved it.

In the bedroom she spied one of the quilts and burst into laughter. "These two quilts!" she said. "Elizabeth and I had quite a spat over them. I had found this wonderful quilt maker in Jordan Bay. And I had ordered two quilts for myself. Then I made the mistake of telling Elizabeth about my find. When I went to ask about the progress of my quilts several months later, the quilt maker told me that Elizabeth had already come and bought them, out from under my nose. I was mad at the quilt-maker for selling them to Elizabeth and I was mad at Elizabeth for buying them. But I got over it, and Elizabeth just thought it was funny."

I think of the three women whose stories intertwine like a design in a quilt: the quilt-maker herself, and the two friends, each with such an adventurous life. We have the quilts by the quirk of a trick, and then later by the kindness of Elizabeth's daughter who left them here for us to keep. They remind me every day of how all the various bits and pieces of our lives are somehow patched together.

Garden between the Forest and the Sea

Our vegetable garden is entering its second year. In June last year we went after the compacted place where a garden had flourished decades earlier. Beneath a tangled layer of grasses and roots we encountered wire, fencing, old fish nets, remnants of plastic tarps, and stones of every size. We added a new deer fence of spruce posts and fish net. It was a late start, but it was a start. All summer and early fall the wind sang through the fish net as I discovered the tiny miracles and disappointments of a vegetable garden.

The miracles outweighed the disappointments. I watched a delirious bee, the baskets on his legs already packed with glowing amber pollen, lurch from flower to flower like a drunk on a pub crawl. "Just one more!" I distinctly heard him say in a buzzing kind of way. And once, a few feet from where I sat weeding, a ruby-throated hummingbird ignored me entirely, so intensely focused was he on the pole beans' scarlet flowers. I learned that a handful of seeds would provide us with six months of sugar snap peas, not to mention the beauty of the flowers that came before the pea pods -- flowers of violet and garnet and azure -- hanging on the vines.

I read that gardening is mostly weeding and heave an inward sigh of relief. I can do weeding. There are so many helpful hints and instructions and lessons for gardening available on the Internet that you could make yourself crazy or paralyzed by trying to take it all in, much less remember it all. Better to just go ahead and make your own mistakes, I think. That way you'll remember them at least. Anyway, it isn't mostly about mistakes and avoiding them. It's mostly about being out there day after day, watching what's going on and taking care of things and letting yourself be amazed.

One thing I learned last summer was that I needed to build stronger trellises. Last year the vines sagged on old lanyard strung between two tall stakes. I tried to stake the stakes, but eventually the strong summer winds and the weight of the vines and leaves and peas made for a mess. This year we will have more trellises, for peas and beans and English cucumber, a particularly nice kind of cucumber that's expensive in the store.

Our new plan is for taller stakes, more deeply buried, with better side supports, and an old herring net for the climbing vines. We found the herring net along the shore past the sheep pen a month or so ago, and Greg went down and got it this weekend. I have marked it off and cut it to size. It's a great net, its weave much heavier than the net we used for the perimeter fence, so easier to work with. And it's beautiful. I especially admire a bright orange line that's been woven into all that lovely teal, some repair done by a fisherman somewhere, sometime.

The stakes are the leftovers from Skipper's lumber milling on the island, so they are from the spruce forest. The net used to hang many fathoms deep below the surface of the sea. Now the worlds of forest and sea will intersect where peas and beans and cucumbers climb from earth to sky.

Regeneration

I have been watching the skeleton forest north of our property since we moved here. Greg has taken down the spruce that used to hide the stone wall boundary and to some extent the forest beyond the wall. Now it is possible to see the slow regeneration taking place within the forest.

Bright green patches of young spruce have established themselves in the midst of all the dead wood. Now, in early spring, you can see the faint pink of small hackmatack and alder, a medium sized maple or two, and the distinguished structure of a tall birch before it has leafed out. The maple and the birch survived the wind storm that toppled their less deeply rooted neighbours, the spruce, several years ago. The hackmatack and alder are among the first deciduous trees to establish themselves after such a destruction.

The land in this forest is one big bog, though it's hard to tell that because of the dense tangle of uprooted trees, old trunks and fallen branches. It's almost impossible to walk through this area. You can do it, but it involves inching your way from fallen log to fallen log, holding onto dead branches that you hope are not going to break off in your hand, and never knowing whether what's beneath your feet will suddenly give way. Beneath the forest are springs and streams and a layer of moss-covered humus, and everywhere a great variety of lichen and fungus.

Though the forest still looks dead, I guess, to someone just glancing at it, I no longer see it that way. I see it as deeply alive and a source of endless admiration.

Good Friday

We spent Good Friday redeeming more of the old farm. Greg continued clearing. He has worked his way down the path toward the lower orchard. Yesterday he got as far as an old well. This well was covered over with dead spruce trunks and brush, and we only happened to glimpse it last summer, a few feet off the path. If they are open, the old wells are dangerous for the sheep. I would not like to have to rescue a sheep who has fallen into one. Soon, Greg will build a wooden frame with a hinged cover. It's on his list. In the meantime we will trust the sheep to keep to the safety of their familiar path and not go wandering off in search of anything new and exciting.

The old wells themselves are not very useful to us, at least not yet. But they were essential to the settlers who built them, who first redeemed this land. Now, no longer practical, they are good for the soul. Their dark glimmer hints of hidden depths beyond the familiar paths.

While Greg worked near the lower path, I continued to clear the field behind the vegetable garden. It was its hundred year clean up, I think. Last year it was covered with spruce trees and its outlines were vague. It was only the memory of a field. Now, the spruce cleared away, you can see the stone wall along the lower road and the two old apple trees that border it. As I raked my way down the wall I found clumps of emerging daffodils near each apple tree. They have been hidden for years, their glory unseen and forgotten, like the wells, and as good for the soul.

Namaste, White-throated Sparrow

I heard the song of this bird soon after we first came to McNutt's Island in early May of 2007. I had heard its song before. But working outside on the island that spring, I heard it for the first time, not as background, but as if I were somehow being drawn into the heart of the world. Be here now, it sang. Be here now.

It left in the fall, and the island stilled in its absence. I longed for it, this bird whose name I didn't yet know. I listened to recorded bird songs, looking for a needle in a haystack. Then somewhere I saw an odd remark about a particular bird whose song was similar to the opening notes of Handel's *Judas Maccabaeus*. And I knew that this was the bird I was searching for. It was the white-throated sparrow.

Then a year ago we heard it sing again, on April 22nd. I could sometimes catch it, perched on a high bough of a spruce tree, singing, but I couldn't see more than its profile. One day it came into the yard and began eating seed. He turned and gazed in my direction while I focused the binoculars and studied him from a few feet away. It had been a holy thing to learn the singer's name, but it felt like entering upon the mystery of mysteries finally to know his face. I was shocked that this perky-looking creature was the tiny portal into such vast beauty. (You might think I would have grasped the gospel idea of The Least of These by now, but, really, it startles me every single time, like I'm falling for the same prank, over and over.)

His song begins with three notes, the second and third in descending intervals, followed by several notes identical to the final introductory note. Sometimes the song ascends rather than descends, and sometimes the preliminary notes are two rather than three. I have also heard a descending three notes, then two triads of quarter notes followed by two eighth notes.

Whatever the variation, the song of the white-throated sparrow holds the essence of the world's soul, and calls you to a place of deepest joy. Greg thought he heard him yesterday, and this morning we watched him masquerading as a commoner and eating seed among the dark-eyed juncos and song sparrows in the side yard. So now we welcome back this most amazing creature. Namaste, I tell him. I bow to that which is holy in you.

First Snake Sighting

Today I met one of the island's snakes along the main road. It was my first snake of the spring, so it was an auspicious meeting. He or she was enjoying the warm gravelly road, reasonably not expecting anybody to come along. The snake graciously allowed me a photo opportunity before it flowed off the road and disappeared completely in the forest as snakes are so good at doing.

According to the Nova Scotia Museum of Natural History web site, the snake I met today was a maritime garter snake. We also have the smooth green snake here; I'm sure it will turn up soon.

In Buddhist tradition the snake is a symbol of wisdom. I find them beautiful and strange, peaceful (though they are not peaceful to their prey, so it depends on your perspective) and graceful. When I meet a snake I am surprised. It wakes me up to the here and now, like the clap of a monk's hands or the sound of a temple bell.

Lazy Bed Potatoes

I kept hearing about growing potatoes in lazy beds. This was a practice developed by poor crofters in Scotland. It was used where the ground was too boggy for cultivation. It wasn't actually lazy, but it was a way to grow food on marginal land. The technique came over to the boggy Maritimes with those immigrants from the old boggy places.

You lay the potato seed on a bed of seaweed straight on the ground, dig trenches down either side of the bed, and then cover the seed with the peaty sod dug from the trenches. It sounded good, especially since so many people around here swore by it. But I didn't think I would have room for potato beds inside the vegetable garden. Then Margot told me about using old fish bait boxes. Here's her recipe: fill an old fish bait box about half-way with a mixture of soil and seaweed. Put the potato seed in, about six or eight seeds to a box. Cover them up with more seaweed. And there you go.

Even though we are not lobstermen, we inherited a few old fish bait boxes (which the lobstermen call fish pans), and I had found more washed up along the shore. So I gathered seaweed from the cove to fill them. I went to the store to buy seed potatoes. But then somebody told me that any old potato would do, as long as you let its eyes sprout. Having to be reminded how to sprout potato seed can make you feel stupid. Like yesterday when I asked Greg whether he thought I could actually fish from my rowboat. It sounded like an exotic proposition at the time: a great conceptual leap. And I suppose it is, in a way, for me at least.

Once again I am reminded of how quickly and easily all sorts of knowledge is lost, from one generation to the next. Neither of us grew up in a teaching family. No useful skills were handed on to us. (And I believe we have passed no useful skills to our own children: maintaining the tradition, as it were, though they are absolutely terrific human beings.) I think our grandparents might have taught us things, but both our families had moved far away from our grandparents, searching for new horizons, new worlds, happily leaving the old behind, embracing the new wonders of frozen food and time-saver meals and all the rest.

I do know that my grandparents grabbled for potatoes, because once my grandmother used the word and then had to explain it to me: it's when you go out to the potato field and dig up a few at a time with your hands, and you must do that carefully lest you destroy the rest. But me, personally? I have never in my life gotten closer to the life cycle of a potato than those childhood experiences of setting one in a jar of water to grow the vines, for no real reason that I can recall.

This is about to change.

Yesterday while we were on the mainland we dropped by Uncle Sid's Market and got a few potatoes each of Yukon Gold, Kennebec, Red Pontiac, and Green Mountain. (Too bad there weren't any blue potatoes at Uncle Sid's. I want some.) I added to this collection a few russets that had helpfully sprouted already, at home. After they've all sprouted I'll plant them in the fish bait boxes and sometime in late summer we will begin to harvest our very own potatoes.

For anybody who has done this before -- and that includes most people we are connected with now, it turns out -- I guess it's no big deal. But for me it's very satisfying. I am continually surprised that you don't have to be an expert to actually get your own food. Slowly we are recovering enough confidence and knowledge to be as competent as the average American before the 1950s.

And with luck eventually we will be able to hold up our heads among the vegetable gardeners and fruit preservers and rabbit snarers and fishermen and deer hunters who live along the shore of Shelburne Harbour, whose parents and grandparents taught them how to do these things, who take all this practical knowledge for granted and maybe don't always realize how truly wonderful a gift they have been given, and who are passing it on their children and grandchildren, because that's what you do.

Tiny Spring

Now is the time to observe the emergence of ferns and mosses that cover the island in bewildering array. Identification will be a multi-year project. The first spring they overwhelmed me and I could only look at them out of the corner of my eye. The second spring I was recovering from my swoon and started to sit up and take notice, but still couldn't figure out how to make any order out of such profligacy, such variety. Now, after two years here, I have settled myself enough to recall that I have a camera and can at least make some record of what I see, so that later -- next winter, say -- I can work on identifying them.

Why should I want to make any order, you may wonder. Why not just wander around and enjoy the sights? I think knowledge helps in recognition. And recognition -- some sense of who this particular Other is, in all its particularity -- helps me be more empathic. Some knowledge -- even a little -- helps me see each creature and plant and rock and cloud and star more clearly, appreciate it more for what it is.

Sedges and rushes, for instance. They are everywhere in the bog below our house and along the path to the shore. I didn't especially notice or like them until I learned something about them. And now I have realized that they are beautiful in their own way.

I did not understand how narrow and rigid was my approach to beauty until I came to the island. Here it is constantly confronted and softened and expanded. It's a little like the process of giving birth: maybe -- I hope -- the birth of a wider, more sympathetic view.

So as I try to learn about them, learn their names and their characteristics, even if it's only a sketchy amount of knowledge, it's a way of entering into a relationship, a way of honouring them. A way of touching the holy, however slightly.

Worm Sanctuary

The garden is now a designated worm sanctuary. My deal with the robins is: you can eat all the worms you want, anywhere you please, except inside the vegetable garden. I haven't bothered to put this deal into writing since I doubt they would take the time to read it, much less sign it. But so far, at least, they seem to be leaving the garden worms alone.

It could be my fluttering anti-robin cloth strips that are actually doing the trick, rather than our little inter-species social contract. I have added the fluttering cloth strips to my defence repertoire, which started with the fluttering deer reminder cloth strips that hang along the outside. The go-away-you-robins strips of cloth hang on twine stretched across the inside of the garden. The twine has gotten a bit saggy since I first tied it up there. Normal-sized people can still walk under it, but it might garrot a really tall person. Greg very kindly says that from the house the whole thing looks like a Greek wedding. I say more a used car lot. It's a very fluttery garden now.

This is the first full year for the vegetable garden. Last summer we got in on the middle of the growing season. I was rather devil-may-care about it back then, figuring that, since it was my first, I had plenty of latitude for error. It's not like I had any standard to live up to.

This year the stakes are higher. Greg has been saying that there's no need for us to buy any vegetables -- ever -- from the grocery store. I think he believes -- touchingly -- that I actually learned something from my experience last summer. This great confidence in my ability makes me feel a little fluttery.

But at least I have begun earlier. I double dug the beds, meeting countless worms in the process and getting a fabulous early harvest of stones. Which were definitely not in those beds last summer. We have built better trellises for the peas and beans and cucumbers, and we took some of the windows we scavenged from the old Roseway Community Hall and made temporary cold frames. I've been using the windows over the seeds, so that the seed-eating birds can't get them. Another line of defence.

So far I've planted peas, turnips, beets, mesclun, chard, spinach, parsnips, fennel, carrots, mustard, shallots, cilantro, zinnias, and a little bit of garlic, to see if you can grow it in the spring. Also sweet peas and that honeysuckle I got last

December from the field next door and a Casa Blanca Lily that I got as a surprise today.

It's early by the calendar and by the average last frost date, which is about three weeks from now, I think. So all this planting could turn out to be pure-dee foolishness. But it's practically spring and out in their sanctuary those really safe worms are doing the boogie-woogie all night long. When I hear that party going on I just can't resist.

Island Sounds

"Did you hear that?" Greg asked me. He looked alert, possibly alarmed. It was one of those sunny days back in April. We were eating lunch outside, at the picnic table. Greg often looks alert but hardly ever alarmed. So his expression caught my attention. "Listen!" he said. "It sounds like a growl." But I couldn't hear anything like that.

We had been talking off and on about the possibility of a bobcat on the island. A couple of our neighbours said they had seen paw prints after the winter snows that belonged to some kind of cat. Could there be a bobcat lurking in the skeleton forest, just beyond that stone wall over there? The sunny day seemed shadowed by something ominous. Not that a bobcat would leap over the wall and attack us. It was just the notion that something potentially dangerous could be so near. But though we both listened, we didn't hear the sound again that day.

Then last week I was walking along the main road toward the government wharf when I heard growling, just like Greg had described it. But now I could tell that the sound was coming from Indian Point. I made my way to the place where there is a little beaten path down from the road to the cove shore and looked toward Indian Point. The tide was going out and six seals were balanced on their rocky resting places beyond the shore, talking to each other. It was their conversation that sounded like growling.

Since the seals have probably been resting on those rocks for hundreds or even thousands of years, I can't imagine what they have left to talk about. The usual stuff, maybe: the weather, the lobster catch, the good old days, the kids. Those conversations can go on forever.

When the weather gets warmer the seals will put away their growls and instead begin to sing, an eerie sound that will float across the island like the summer fog. For now the growling is no longer alarming to us. It has become something we listen for, and are glad to hear.

Quiet Garden

The garden is so quiet that I can hear a single bumblebee wending her way through it. She flies in through the fish net fence and bumbles about before flying out again. She knocks her head against the net as she exits, but doesn't seem fazed. Outside the fence a bee-feast of miniscule violets lies sprinkled across the grass, pale blue and creamy white. The last of the daffodils that border the garden are nodding, nectar deep inside their gold trumpets where only a bee can reach.

I turned over the next-to-last bed this week. It will be for squash when the soil is warm enough. The biggest worm I have ever seen lives in this bed. He is more than a foot long, though he was in too much of a hurry to let me stretch him out and measure him. I found the fattest worm I have ever seen in the same bed, as thick as my thumb. The most beautiful worm in the world may be in here, too. Possibly this bed is a designated zone for prize worms. I would like to give them an award for splendour. Instead, I walk around the garden and peer into every bed to admire the castings all the worms -- big and small, prize-winning and not -- leave behind as they silently munch their way through the soil.

I planted the seeds too early but I was lucky. Here it is nearly Victoria Day and there has been no late frost after all. Orderly rows of tiny leaves -- turnips, beets, spinach, peas, chard, mustard, carrots -- have emerged, in spite of too much rain. It is slow going. These are seeds, after all, not seedlings ready to pop out of their little plastic packs. Hidden in the earth among the worms, the seeds unfold and stretch upward. I hover and scrutinize the beds each day, wanting signs of progress, visible evidence that it's all going to be okay. But there is nothing for me to see until, one day, there is. My vegetable book tells me that the parsnips may take a month to break the soil. After my eager bumbling beginning the garden has taken me in hand and is giving me a make-up course in patience as it quietly spins water and soil and light into gold.

Dangerous Garden

As soon as the seedlings began to emerge I saw silvery traces of slime in the garden beds. The tiny turnip leaves were already being chewed. Slugs. I had read about setting out beer traps so on Saturday evening -- a perfect time for a party, or a drowning, however you prefer to imagine it -- I took matters into my own hands and did just that. I used the dregs of Greg's latest home brew, not wanting to waste the real thing on such undiscerning drinkers.

My organic gardening book warned that I needed to build a complicated contraption or risk the collateral damage of beneficial insects. I ignored the advice, thinking it overly scrupulous. I set out plastic lids turned upside down and filled them with beer dregs. I imagined the slugs, under cover of darkness, slithering eagerly into the lids and enjoying a brief moment of drunken ecstasy before permanent oblivion closed upon them. They would die happy I thought, or at least in a stupor.

But when I checked the lids this morning there were no slugs. Instead I found four beetles deep in the brew. Disgusted with myself, I dumped three of them into the garden path and brought one into the house to identify it. Margot and Dave and Skipper and Dylan were coming for breakfast, so I carefully placed the beetle on top of the book case. I thought a drowned beetle wasn't the most appetizing sight for guests, even if they are island neighbours who are used to a number of conditions not encountered in the polite world. I would look him up later. Then, getting ready for breakfast, I forgot about him.

"A bug just flew off the shelf," Dylan announced during breakfast. It's true what they say: Dylan does have sharp eyesight. When I investigated it turned out that he was right. The bug -- miraculously revived -- now lay on the floor, on his back, waving his legs. After breakfast I identified him and put him back in the garden. I noticed that his three fellow partiers were not where I had dumped them earlier. They must have dragged themselves home with serious headaches.

My tiny drunks are ground beetles, among the vast crew of beneficial insects you really don't want to lose. They are, literally, do-gooders. They were on my side all along! Or, more precisely, on the side of light and life and tiny turnip greens, which I like to think of as my side even though obviously that's not always true. They are ancient animals whose favourite menu includes slugs, snails, cutworms and root maggots. Sometimes they eat an earthworm, too, but nobody's perfect.

I hope I have learned my lesson. From now on I'll depend on the mercy of ground beetles, sober and alert, patrolling the garden while I sleep, being good for the garden even though I don't deserve it.

Rearranging the Universe

I have been filling an old wooden cart with stones, so that Greg can hitch the cart to the ATV and then take the stones down to the path that runs through our bog. He stabilized the path about a year ago by dumping stones on it. But it's a bog. It will always need more stones. Luckily for us, we have them.

When we moved here two years ago, Skipper made us a driveway from the lower road to our house. On top of the new driveway he laid down stones from the cobble beach. Afterward, there were cobbles left over, and in all the excitement they got dumped on top of an old stone wall. Now my job is to take the beach cobble away from the stone wall. I'm editing the wall, maybe. Or restoring it, but I think that's a word that claims too much for what I'm doing. I want the old stones to look at rest again, that's all.

You might not think how easy it is to see the difference between these two kinds of stones. The old wall is composed of stones from beneath the earth, home-grown, gathered up and pitched to thigh-high more than a hundred years ago. These stones are pretty big, mostly. The kind you would want to clear out of your field if you were going to plant anything there. They are dark grey and brown, softened with decades of lichen and moss. For stones, they have a kind of visual quality of softness. They come across as settled stones, stones with roots. These are the Old Fellers' stones.

Then, on top of the old wall, are beach stones. They come from away, in a way. They would never have gotten here on their own. They are varied: white, speckled with black, round and smooth as gull eggs; pale grey or darker, sharply edged; golden bronze and stippled. They are smaller than the Old Fellers' stones. Tossed by wave action onto the island's shore, they could have come from anywhere in the world, really. They are beautiful in their own right, but they just don't seem to belong. Maybe in another hundred years they would fit in here. But we have a better use for them, right now. Willy-nilly, they are moving on.

While I'm working a single snake has emerged from her lair within the old wall. She watches me for a while, then lays her head along a warm stone and basks, soaking up a pale spring sun. She looks calm and peaceful, even when I get an arm's length from her. We keep an eye on each other the whole time that

I am loading the cart. She can probably trace her local roots back to the time of the Old Fellers themselves. But of course she has no need to. She knows where she belongs.

Scientists now think there may be a universal consciousness embodied at the cellular level and including all material – not just what we have generally thought of as living things, but the inanimate as well. In our narrowly rational twentieth century framework we thought that animism was a child-like thing, to be outgrown or overcome. But the mystics have always recognized the world's immanent spirit, the presence of life force in all things, even a stone. So the universe is constantly rearranged, sometimes very slowly, and sometimes as quickly as I can toss bits of it into the cart.

Rainy Days

Two days of chilly rain remind me that the seasons do not turn upon our needs. Spring is happening out there, but on its own terms, which sometimes coincide with ours but sometimes not. In the midst of rain and wind the earth stretches and warms for its summer dance. The light grows longer, buttercups arise. The ferns unfold, and repair a broken patch of dead forest with their greenery.

Luckily we still have dry wood for the stove, library books to read, and jeans to mend.

I am not good at sewing, but I can patch a rip in a pair of jeans. It isn't false economy to keep Greg's old work jeans in repair. He's hard on his jeans, snagging them on this and that. And being six feet and five inches tall, and that mostly legs, he is such an odd size that Frenchy's does not have jeans for him. To replace the ones he wears every day would mean buying something new and not cheap. I'm being practical here, not romantic or sentimental.

My patching is inept and slow. I think of all the women of the past who have kept their household's clothing in good repair over years of wear and tear. I imagine they never sat down without a needle and thread in hand. I think of the fishermen mending their nets, of old farm wagons and machinery kept in service for decades. How, I wonder, did the act of mending become so out of date, the art become so lost?

The patched jeans have a certain something that new jeans lack, though I wouldn't go so far as to say exactly what that certain something might be. They are evidence that things both momentous and mundane are always falling apart and breaking. At some times -- in spring, for example -- the world goes about repairing itself, gracefully and on its own terms. With my uneven stitches I join the dance, however awkwardly.

Lamb Watching

Greg and I are spying on the lambs. It's a cool, rainy day anyway, good for being inside. We walk from window to window with the binoculars and the camera, observing but unobserved. The lambs born first show off their superiority: they butt the smaller ones, who sometimes butt back, and sometimes just settle down on the ground, or run off to nurse. The older lambs like to be king of the mountain, and climb up onto any higher level they can find: a granite boulder caught here since the ice age, the concrete platform of the solar tracker, a wicker chair. They butt the others off: get out of here; this is mine!

There's nothing these lambs meet up with that does not incite their curiosity. They must explore wood piles, daffodils, chairs, tree trunks, propane tanks, ATV wheels, whatever is in their way. It's all new! They literally gambol about. They are gambolling distilled. They leap off the ground from all four feet, they bounce across the grass like the world is their trampoline, they jump over each other. They are so new that I can see their entire bodies, their muscles and bones and inward shapes, not yet layered over with meat or fat or wool, drying umbilical cords still dangling beneath them.

They are so new that they firmly believe their own mother is the most beautiful mother in the world, even if a more objective observer could say she was a bit mangy. Then, suddenly overtaken by so much newness, they lie down and rest for a while.

The Other Rabbit

Last week I heard an urgent, terrorized screaming coming from the direction of the lower road. I was close by, near the garden, and when I got to the road I saw a mink and a rabbit intertwined, writhing in furious mortal battle.

I should not have, I think now, but I intervened. I threw rocks at the mink until it ran away, and then Greg came and caught the wounded rabbit, which we took home and cared for, haplessly, awkwardly, but could not, of course, either comfort or save. It was terrified of us. It was the inhabitant of another world, something entirely wild, and in spite of our best intentions we could not reach across that boundary.

The rabbit was not alone when the mink attacked it. Another rabbit was with it, or nearby. While the rabbit was fighting for its life the other rabbit sat in the middle of the road, about fifty feet beyond, and watched. When I arrived and started throwing rocks at the mink, the other rabbit continued to sit in the middle of the road and watch. After the mink ran away and Greg crawled through the underbrush and caught the wounded rabbit and we began to carry it toward the house, I looked back. The other rabbit had not moved. It was still watching.

I wonder about the relationship between the two rabbits, what they were to each other. I can't know how, but they were connected. Nor can I know what the other rabbit was seeing, from its animal perspective and watching on the other side, beyond the event, further on up the road. But it was seeing something.

It felt wrong to separate the two of them, to take the dying rabbit away from its familiar world, its watching friend or brother or mate. But of course the mink would have returned -- did in fact return, before we had even left the scene -- to drag its dinner away. Anyway, by then we were well along in our unconsidered course of action, and we would see it through.

When I first saw the attack my impulse was to do something. But I hope the next time I come upon such a bloody, wild moment I will remember the other rabbit. In silence and stillness the other rabbit witnessed the whole terrifying event. It did not run away and hide. What it did was not second best. What it did was not nothing. What it did was, I now think, more right than what I did.

It's an image for me of something holy, of something, even, like prayer: the other rabbit, in the sun-lit road, watching the whirlwind of activity that was hungry mink, desperate rabbit, us; watching the little tragedy unfold, holding it all within its steady gaze.

History of Rhubarb

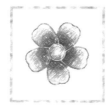

When we first came to this place we discovered a forlorn little clump of rhubarb. It was scruffy and choked with weeds, emerging along the edge of the ghostly vegetable garden, among the daffodils and June lilies. It was the remnants of the Old Fellers' rhubarb, going back, we guessed, a hundred years or so. It was the sort of thing you wanted to look away from. But there it was, still coming up, even though it had been years since anyone had laid eyes on it. You had to admire its fortitude. But we could not pay any attention to something as slight as rhubarb during those first months when we were so anxious about our old leaky house and the coming winter.

Last spring we still had not yet turned to restoring the garden. But we watched as the rhubarb began to appear again, between the return of the white-throated sparrow and the birth of the new lambs. Greg was a big fan of rhubarb. It was a taste of his New England roots. And now it seemed that in moving to the island we had lucked into a rhubarb heaven. Skipper's father, the island's lighthouse keeper for so many years, had been a serious grower of rhubarb. He swore by the application of ash. Captain Van had died, but his rhubarb patches continued to flourish each year behind his house on the mainland, in Gunning Cove, where he had retired.

One day Skipper brought us a big bag full of the long red stems, huge green leaves flopping. Greg searched his cookbooks and announced that only in my old Farm Journal cookbook could he find a recipe he liked, for rhubarb cobbler. It was well received among our adult neighbours, but too tart for the kids. Some of the Van Buskirk extended family were fond of making rhubarb juice from the stalks, boiling them down to a concentrate to which they could add other ingredients. It seemed a practical and delicious use of so much rhubarb. But Greg's commitment to cobbler was unyielding.

More and more rhubarb appeared at our kitchen door, mostly with Skipper. Then Charlie's wife Queenie sent over some rhubarb from her own patch, telling Greg that now he would see that the rhubarb from the hamlet of Churchover, two miles up the road, was much better than Gunning Cove rhubarb.

Last summer we finally returned the old vegetable garden to a semblance of its former self. We dug up the Old Fellers' scraggly rhubarb and replanted it in its new bed. In the fall we dug up a big clump from Queenie's garden in Churchover and added that too.

The other day I went out and cut the first of our rhubarb. We got enough for Greg to make a rhubarb pudding cake that's sort of like strawberry shortcake. Delicious.

There was a time when rhubarb was the anticipated first fruit of spring after a long dreary season of mud and turnips and old potatoes. And it was more than just the rhubarb itself, as wonderful as it was. Its arrival contained the promise of strawberries, and after that raspberries and gooseberries and currants and blueberries, and then apples and pears and cranberries and deep purple concord grapes -- all from right where you lived, your own garden or your orchard, or from someplace nearby that you knew as well as you knew your own. For us, that time has come again.

Song of the Toad

Last night a tiny, dark trilling wafted into the house. The toads were back! I felt a rising sense of good cheer. I had been missing them and wondering when they would emerge from their winter's hibernation. After only two years here I have learned that life is not quite the same when the toads are asleep. After the toads wake up the whole island seems more interesting, more lively, more full of surprises. And now it's about to get that way again.

But first they sing, the males calling to the females with their musical trills. And so last night we listened to their songs floating up from the bog: tenor, baritone, bass. The bog, I'll bet, is a romantic meeting place on a fine spring night with its red sliver of new moon and canopy of twinkling stars, if you are a toad in search of love.

The island is filled with these humble creatures, though they are easy to overlook. They sound quite debonair in the bog, of course. But then when you meet them later on, on land, they are so remarkably slow that they can seem a little dim-witted, like clods of earth suddenly come to life.

As much as you are surprised to see them they are generally dumbfounded to see you. What could that be, they wonder, staring at you. And while they ought to be moving on, lest you be planning toad soup for supper, they take a while to gather their thoughts.

Once last summer I interrupted a toad when I moved a rock -- his rock, it turned out to be -- along the side of the house. He slowly made for the wall of the house, which he tried to climb up with a sort of frantic slowness. Eventually, with great perseverance, he made his way several feet along the edge of the cedar shakes -- occasionally trying out the wall-climbing option again -- until he found a small entrance into the darkness beneath the house, and disappeared.

Two toads took up housekeeping at opposite ends of the new garden last summer. There was one near the grape arbour: Toad of the North. And the second near the asparagus patch: Toad of the South. I hoped they would come back to the garden again this year, so I have built little toad houses for them, of rocks and boards, with a toad-sized pond in the front yard for swimming. I hope it's all to their liking and not too gauche.

How toads find their houses I do not know, any more than how bats or martins find the houses people make for them. It seems extravagant to hope that in the whole wide world a toad might come upon the very house you had made for him. But then why shouldn't it work like that? After all, many will hear the toad singing tonight: the lambs, the sparrows, the mice, the herons, us. But only his own true love will follow his song and search slowly through the dark spring bog until she finds him.

Washing the Windows

I've finished washing the windows in the kitchen and living room. Last fall, in an effort to reduce the inherent windiness of an old clapboard house, Greg caulked the wooden storm windows in place. So taking off the storms this spring has been a slower process. Each storm window has been made specifically for a particular window. And each one has its own quirks, which I am beginning to know.

After the storm windows were off and safely stored in the shed, I washed the windows. Even with our woodstove going all winter long, there was no dust or grime to speak of on the windows. But after I have removed the storm windows and washed all the panes with vinegar and water, the windows sparkle.

Most of the windows still have the old original panes with bubbles and wavy glass. If you sit across the room and look out through the windows the world outside dissolves into small discrete Impressionist views, each small rectangle slightly off kilter from its neighbours. A few panes of new glass have been installed over the years to replace old ones that have broken. When you look through a pane of new glass you see a world that is literal, factual: sky, sea, tree. Within the same window, the views through the older panes slide this way and that, like water rippling in the cove on a quiet day. When you look through the original glass you see a world that's open to interpretation.

The kitchen windows are quite small, and low. Visitors comment on how small they are. Really, if you want to look outside while you are in the kitchen you will need to bend down, or sit down at the kitchen table, which is Greg's special quiet late afternoon place for drinking a beer or a mug of tea and planning his menus or making his lists for trips to town, and looking outside. If I go into the kitchen while he's sitting there, he growls. In earlier times people did not care for views as we do. If you had to get your living the hard way, by going out to sea in a little boat, you didn't want to sit looking at the sea when you were safe at home.

So the windows in the living room are a good size considering when they were built, in about 1858, and considering that this was not an elegant house like those in the Town of Shelburne, but a simple fisherman's cottage on a remote island. When you sit in the living room, because we made three smaller rooms into one room, you can look out in three directions. The weather here can be very dramatic. Last night -- an undramatic night -- the sunset was pink and gold and copper and grey over the water on the western side while night darkened into deep indigo on the eastern side.

I guess if you were going to build a house from scratch in a beautiful and wild place like this you might be tempted to put in a room with all glass, so you could see everything that was going on. When we first moved here we thought we might eventually add such a glassed-in room. As it is, a heron flies past and you catch a glimpse in one window, then a millisecond later another glimpse, then a third. You don't see the heron in flight, really: only brief bits and pieces of it. The world outside comes to us in fragments, never whole.

I have read (in *A Pattern Language*) that small windows, or windows with many small panes, are actually more pleasing for people to look through than large expanses of glass. It's the contrast, if I remember right, between the sturdy walls and upright framework that keep us sheltered safe inside and those brief, defined glimpses of something intense and vast and wild, something that beckons us but also humbles us, outside, beyond.

Cedar Waxwings Flocking

Last week Greg and I were admiring the bees among the apple blossoms when Skipper and Dylan happened along, looking for lambs. "There's a cedar waxwing in that apple tree," Dylan announced. I told you he has good eyesight. He knows his birds, too. Once Dylan had pointed them out I could see a few cedar waxwings along the branches of the apple tree. I had never seen them before, but maybe that was because I hadn't known to look for them. That kind of thing happens to me a lot.

Later that day I counted nine of them as they rose from the branches of the little apple tree in the front yard and zoomed off together. In late afternoon I sat in the garden and watched as dozens of cedar waxwings took over the apple tree that might or might not be a Transcendent Crab. They waved up and down along the flimsiest of branches, and made short excursion flights from one part of the tree to another, all the while enjoying each other's company. These birds are extroverts. I could often count as many as half a dozen within a few feet of each other.

Their beauty is hard to describe. To call them grey and yellow does not do justice to the subtle blending of shades and sheen along their breasts. Their top knot is like a cardinal's and gives them a distinctive profile so that once you have heard of them they are easy to spot. And the soft pink and white of the apple blossoms complements their colouring. Apple trees in blossom were made for cedar waxwings, and the other way around.

But the most distinguishing characteristic of these birds is their gluttony. Most birds that visit the apple trees are looking for insects in the bark and finding their food the hard way, pecking for it, bug by bug. Not these guys. They were perched all over that maybe Transcendent Crab actually eating the blossoms. They stuffed the petals into their mouths like there was no tomorrow. I think they could have stripped that tree down to its leaves before sunset if they had felt like it, but fortunately for the tree they heard about some even better tree somewhere else and flew off together to look for it, like a crowd of beautiful shiny bar-hoppers looking for a livelier party in some other neighbourhood.

Rainy Days Again

This is the second of three or four consecutive rainy days. I woke up to thunder this morning and we have heard it off and on all morning. The temperature is about 10 Celsius. Spring has been mostly wet and cool, with bright sunny days only now and then. I think it is just the nature of life so close to the sea.

Yesterday the rain didn't begin in earnest until afternoon so we were both able to go about our projects. Greg had chipped a big pile of apple branches the day before so I added the wood chips to the garden paths and defined the space below the grape arbour. I plan to put an old wooden chair under the arbour and then I will sit out there on a hot sunny day and look at the garden. If we ever have a hot sunny day. I found a small wooden cable spool on the shore that I plan to lug up to the garden, so there will be a little table next to the chair. It will be idyllic. Maybe I'll have two chairs in case someone comes by and wants to sit there, too.

The grape arbour seems to be doing well this year. I think it's what is called a Fox Grape, which is a wild grape. My reference book says that a wild grape vine may live for well over a century. I wonder how old this one is. Last year we trained its huge old stem to the new structure, and pruned it. There were no grapes at all. But I am hopeful for this year's harvest, even if we only get a bit of juice. And I'd like to preserve some of the leaves this year so we can have stuffed grape leaves later on.

We have begun to taste the garden in spite of so much cool wet weather. When I thinned the turnips Greg sautéed the thinnings in garlic and oil. We've also had tiny mustard greens mixed into a salad. And he is using the herbs that are already flourishing in the little narrow kitchen garden next to the house: oregano, thyme, mint, sage. But we will go slowly with eating the greens until the plants are better established, in another month or so. Or maybe never, unless the sun can shine a bit more.

The rain varies from drenching to drizzle to fine mist. The harbour waters match the pale grey of the clouds, and whoosh in sheets away from the shore, but there's hardly any wind. The shore across the harbour is remote, grey, veiled. A few of the ewes and their lambs are huddled beneath the hackmatack trees. The rams stand silently staring at nothing, or lie about.

The rams have discovered the bird seed. One of them butted the pole the feeder sits on, and all the seed spilled out onto the ground. They were delighted with themselves. Greg went out and spoke to them but they were not at all remorseful.

Leroy told us while he was here on Sunday that he raised the two North Country Cheviot rams himself, and that The Major was raised by a veterinarian in Lunenberg. We call the two Cheviots Balzac and Bertie. Lately the ram elders have allowed the fourth ram, the young one with the long tail, to join them. This season has been his first foray into the world of ram adulthood, and we've only seen him moping about on his own until now. Greg has named him Fred. The four of them slouch about the island, a little lazy gang, their work here finished.

Messing About in Boats

I have a rowboat, called *Roseneath* after the old name for McNutt's Island. I believe every boat here, no matter how small, has a name. *Roseneath* was Greg's birthday present to me a year and a half ago. She was an old wooden rowboat that Skipper fixed up. Last summer I rowed around in the cove on almost any fine day. She was a little bunged up by the time we pulled her out of the water just before a gale, sometime last fall. All winter she lay overturned on a couple of logs down by the dock.

This spring Greg set about to get her ready for the summer. He filled in a hole in the stern where she had knocked about on the rocks at low tide. He scraped, sanded, caulked, primed and painted her, inside and out, and stained and re-varnished the ribbands and the plug. The only thing he didn't do was repaint the rose and the name on her bow. Garrett had painted those, and they are too beautiful for anybody else to do over. He added some old lobster buoys that he had found along the shore and painted. These are little fenders now, so *Roseneath* won't go bumping against the dock and get herself all scraped up.

Since she's made of wood she's a heavy boat. So we asked Skipper and Dylan to help launch her for the summer. The four of us carried her into the water at high tide, Greg and Skipper lifting and Dylan and I providing balance and guidance, fore and aft. On land *Roseneath* is a heavy, awkward boat. But once she's in the water she becomes something graceful.

Then I rowed down to wave at Margot and Dave, who are working on their camp. Dylan rowed Little Star out into the cove and I admired his very fast rowing. Good thing we weren't having a race. Then Dylan picked up his cousin Susannah and rowed her about in the cove, slowly. Susannah is six. "I've done this before," she informed me across the water as she sat gravely in the bow.

I left them rowing near the sheep pen and rowed toward the point, that rocky bar that defines the cove's southern end. I could see a few gull chicks wobbling along the shore while their extended family zoomed over my head and made loud noises to scare me away. I watched the terns wheeling and crying at the end of the point. I had not known whether they were nesting there yet. But they gave themselves away. A raft of eiders further out in the harbour, startled, took flight.

It was such a beautiful day that I rowed on, to Indian Point, where I saw three sheep quietly grazing, and a heron. Several lobster pots have been set here, and I carefully rowed around their bright coloured lines and gently floating buoys. If I leaned over the edge of the boat I could see underwater meadows of rockweed, golden and green, waving back and forth.

Foggy Garden

It has been a long slow spring in the garden. I guess this is a typical spring for gardens along the southwest shore of Nova Scotia. After all, it is the Atlantic Ocean we are on the edge of: a force of nature there's no point going up against. We have had more days of rain than not. Plenty of those rains have been deluges, the kind where you lie in bed at night listening to the rain pouring out of the sky and thinking about those little seeds all being washed away to Kingdom Come. Then you wait until the soil has drained enough to plant again.

The soil has warmed, gradually and slowly, but we have not yet had many brilliantly bright days. They will come, but not until August and September, I think. In summer this is a cool and foggy place. I'm not complaining about that. It's truly lovely. It just means you need to think about the garden a bit differently.

A few more days of sunlight would move things along, but the weather forecast is for more rain and cloud. "He's giving rain," is how folks around here put it. But they don't seem to get too exercised about what he may or may not be giving or withholding. They have made peace with his capricious ways.

This year I have learned that the number of days from germination to harvest listed on the seed packet is the number of days in some ideal world that contains the exactly correct proportions of water, warmth and sunlight. There's nothing wrong with that. It's just that it doesn't tell you much about your very own garden in its very own situation. And it's a set-up for frustration. That often happens when you measure reality against an ideal world, I think.

The garden is teaching me to let go of my expectations and soak up the reality. This foggy patch of soil is a thing of beauty, to me anyway. It's filled now with slowly growing beans and beets and turnips and chard, peppers and leeks, parsnips and shallots and cabbages and squash. There are eight fish bait boxes of lazy bed potatoes that are overflowing with luxurious green leaves. And yesterday I found a tiny new toad at the end of a row of turnips.

World of Wind

For the past several days a strong westerly wind has blown across the island. The days are sparkling with sunlight on deep teal waters and skies that are a correspondingly intense blue, sometimes filled with racing nimbus and cumulus clouds that turn the day from cold to hot to cold again so that everything's changing, all the time, all day. Dramatic weather is one of Nova Scotia's great overlooked and unsung gifts to the world.

Today is the last day of lobster season for this district. Boats are picking up their traps and returning to the mainland. It's a challenging enterprise, bringing in a mass of heavy traps stacked high and filling the deck of the boat. A calmer day would make the effort easier, but there it is. Maybe they will hoist their stern sails, catch a tail wind, and save a bit of diesel on the run home.

In the garden I have almost finished amending the soil in the raised beds. I forked it over a few times until the tines of the fork sank down like butter, then added my half-baked compost and let it sit on top. Before I plant I'll work that compost in. There's not much dirt in this part of Nova Scotia. Rocks, yes. Moss, yes. Swampy boggy cold wet stuff lying just beneath the surface even in places where the ground looks firm enough, definitely yes.

But our vegetable garden sits where the early island settlers had theirs, I think. They did the hard work. And so the soil is good to begin with, though it was compacted when we first began. Now I'm building on the cumulative effort of the past hundred and fifty years, adding another layer.

As I work the wind sings through the mesh of the herring net that fences the garden. This magical net can catch fish in the sea and stop deer and sheep from invading the garden. But it does not even try to hold back the wind.

Season of Grace

Introduction: Looking at Starfish

I spied starfish near the government wharf yesterday, and climbed down beneath the wharf to see if I could find more. They live in the middle zone of rocky shore habitat, where they feed on barnacles and periwinkles.

Even on this foggy day the moving water is filled with light. The particular beauty of each stone is revealed as it absorbs and reflects the sky. The starfish are luminous, as if they contained a tiny bit of celestial starlight though their home is here, in this hidden place between the tides.

The light-filled starfish make me think of the Quakers' practice of holding someone in the Light. It is a kind of wordless prayer for another. I wonder if this is the secret task of the starfish: to hold the world in the Light.

The Elementary Life

When the children were little they had a small boxed set of Laurent de Brunhoff's *Babar* books. The set was called something like *The Elements*. Each of the four tiny books was devoted to the discovery of an Aristotelian element -- earth, fire, water, air -- through the explorations and experiences of the elephants and their friends. In Babar's world the elements were as fanciful and enchanting as the king's own green suit. But out amongst the grown-ups the elements were abstract concepts: not really there. We had more important things to think about. I sometimes remember the sense of intricate wonder contained in those little books as I am slowly introduced to the elementary life.

Now that the daily provision of heat is not an issue, we have turned to the production and storing up of food. Most of next winter's wood pile is split and stacked, Greg's work of March and April. Since early May I've spent most of my time working in the garden or the greenhouse, getting ready for the brief growing season that is almost upon us. I think mostly in terms of growing what we can freeze for the winter. Meanwhile, Greg has become adept at pre-dawn visits to the gill net and at gutting the fish he finds there. He's at work on a small chicken coop in hopes that we can begin to have a few chickens after all. He is brewing more beer. All of this is absorbing and complex, time-consuming and labour-intensive. It's not so simple. But with each season, I think, we inch closer to the mysteries of the elements.

Time plays its part as well. I missed lots of what was really going on when I lived a speeded-up, multi-tasking, over-developed life. Because lots of what is really going on either changes in an instant, like a heron flying over, or takes eons, like the waves against the rock. My normal mode wasn't tuned into the extremes. Then there is the subtle unfolding and fullness and waning of each season, which I am only slowly beginning to recognize. I didn't realize that I was missing so much, though -- how could I know what I wasn't aware of? I just thought that life was somehow narrower than I wanted it to be, and I didn't want it to end like that as I got older, narrowing and narrowing.

I've been worried about our snake population, but as the weather has warmed up I've started seeing more of them. One or two are in the vegetable garden when I go up in the mornings. And yesterday a tiny twitch of a bright green fern bank revealed the hidden presence of a toad slowly making his way away from me. The snakes and toads are themselves fanciful, out of a children's story, and might even wear suits on occasion, though I have not yet observed it, and possibly that special occasion does not often arise. Snakes and toads are mysteries too, enchanting, earthily elemental, present yet elusive. Happy the person who is fortunate enough -- and slow enough --to notice them.

Wells

We had been concerned about the possibility of lambs and sheep falling into some of the old wells. So in the past few days Greg has built new covers for three of them. He is slowly using up all the old lumber that was still around the property. When we completed the restoration of the house we had a big pile of old lumber for various future projects. There's hardly any of it left now.

As far as we know there are five wells. Four of them could be as old as the first settlers here, more than two centuries ago. They are traditionally-built spring wells lined with rocks. Elizabeth Hyde, the former owner, knew the location of every well and tried to restore them and keep them usable. Like everyone who had lived here before her, Elizabeth did not have running water. For her daily use she drew water from the well in front of the house. The other wells were near the garden, along the path to the fish house, and in the bog near the lower orchard.

We used the front yard well as soon as we arrived two years ago. Greg replaced the frame and built a new cover right away, and it was our water source for washing dishes and clothes and ourselves that first summer, until our new well was dug.

We drew the water up with a pail. I learned how to clear the water's surface by tapping it with the bottom of the pail before dipping the pail beneath the water. I had never drawn water from a well before that summer. We heated the water on the Coleman camp stove which was all we had at the time. I washed clothes and dishes at a table in the front yard beneath the apple tree. We hung Elizabeth's shower bucket from a branch of the oak tree for indescribably wonderful showers.

The new well is near the old garden well, where there are several springs. It's about eight or ten feet deep and consists of a stack of concrete rings set on top of pebble and cobble filtration. The water is pumped from the well through pipe laid underground to the cellar, and then into the house. A portion of that ditch for the pipe, about twenty feet or so, had to be dug with a shovel because it ran along the side of the house and then to the cellar, in too narrow a space for a back hoe, and I'm glad to say that I was the ditch digger. The pump is electric, and runs on the energy we get from sun and wind. So we have running water in the kitchen and bathroom sinks, the shower and the washing machine, and we have a toilet that flushes.

Now that we have running water, we no longer have a practical use for the old wells. They're like the pottery shards we sometimes find around the place: quiet reminders of the people who were here long before us, who found the springs and dug the wells by hand and lined them with stones they pulled out of the earth and carried from around the property and so, with great effort and skill, made this place their own.

A Narrow Escape on Mid-summer's Day

We celebrated Mid-summer's Day with a visit to a secret bog we found in the spring. I wanted to see whether orchids grew there, too, since we spied our first orchid -- dragon's mouth -- in another bog we discovered on Mid-summer's Day a year ago.

In this new-to-us bog we found dragon's mouth aplenty, and also another kind of orchid, called grass pink. They are small shy orchids and you have to look carefully to find them hidden in boggy shaded places, among the bayberry and holly. Come further in! they whispered shyly to us, and so, spell-bound, we did.

Many enchanting sights appeared as we walked deeper and deeper into the bog. Blue iris winked like jewels. The northern pitcher plant's flower glowed red. We peered, entranced, at its charmingly sinister basal cups filled with water, where poor unsuspecting creatures are lured in and drowned, while the bog fairies hover nearby and laugh. Nobody ever said bog fairies were nice.

After wandering around the bog and almost getting sucked down into the netherworld, we went a different way out. Then we got so lost. Because ferns had overgrown the trail we found last spring; more trees had fallen; everything had been turned around and rearranged and obscured, the better to lure poor unsuspecting creatures like us. Though, really, we ought to know better by now.

Luckily for us the mosquito repellent Greg had bought at the Dollar Store has an actual compass embedded in its top (also a whistle, though who would have heard us? And it was a very soft whistle. But still: good thought.) Without the mosquito repellent compass we might still be wandering around in circles in the forest. We saw the osprey nest from several different angles, that's all I'm saying. Eventually we came to the eastern passage. Really, I can't imagine how we got there.

Then more slogging through deceptively smooth-looking fern covered fields and broken deadfall where I'm sure I heard the sounds of elvish snickering, until at last we crossed the path that leads to the main road, and -- just like that -- we found ourselves transported from the realm of mid-summer magic back to reality.

When Seals Play Games

The harbour seals were singing while I rowed in the cove this morning. I think fog inspires them to heights of sealish melody. I rowed toward Indian Point, where they often loll about on some exposed rocks at low tide. I decided to creep up on them by rowing backward -- by which I mean my stern was going forward, which is backward, if you get my drift. It is an awkward way to row, but it let me face them as I approached.

Now and then I stopped rowing entirely and drifted, all the time coming closer and closer, ever so stealthily. I was quite proud of how well I was sneaking up on them, until they slid off their rocks and disappeared beneath the water. They had been watching me the whole time, I guess.

I changed my strategy then. I rowed boldly into the wide cove above Indian Point and rested my oars and sat. Dark heads began to emerge from beneath the water to look at me. I counted eight. It's a curious experience to wait for seals to show themselves. If they want, they will let you see them. Also if they want, they can look at you without being seen. They can come up, look you over, and disappear again all without your knowing it, even if you are sitting right in the middle of them. Several times I heard a splash close behind me and turned as fast as I could, to see nothing but leftover ripples and a few air bubbles. It felt like a game of hide and seek, or maybe blind man's bluff. Whatever the game was, they had the home advantage.

Afternoon Light

The sky was cloudless and blue all day long, and the light shimmered off placid harbour water. I spent the day in the sun-filled garden, mostly weeding. I dug up a row of chewed-up wretched chard and put the leek seedlings there instead. It's much better now. I wonder if I am already so used to the garden that I'm forgetting how miraculous it is. Those beets, for instance -- they were seeds. And now beneath the soil they are real live beets, glowing red.

A robin has built a lovely nest in the grape arbour. Her choice of nesting spots itself was brilliant. What's not to love about being nestled among the grape leaves? But she seems to think that every time I go in or out of the garden I am a threat to her. So then she must make a ruckus and fly off, and perch along the top of the fence and glare at me. This is a good example of over-reacting. I am sorry for her, but I hope she figures out that she can sit on her nest in peace and safety and I can work in the garden at the same time.

But I digress. I meant to write about the afternoon light that's dancing along the living room floor. It is after seven o'clock here and the sun is still glorious. I am sitting at the wooden table where I write to you, at my laptop, looking out through the front door at the apple tree and the sun and the water. I hope that peace and safety surround you, and that this moment is touched with light.

View from the Cove

The water is blue silk today, and so this morning I rowed out to the middle of the cove. Then I sat in the boat and looked all around and watched the morning unfold.

A dignified seal took the air and swam about nearby, calmly ignoring me. I could hear his relations singing across the harbour, from their favourite ledges, which are actually named Seal Ledges on some maps. I think the False Passage seals have been here since time began. It's possible they own the water here, although I don't imagine they have any deeds to prove it.

The water was so clear that, as I rowed, I could see the cove's silty bottom beyond the rocky shoreline, long strands of seaweed undulating in waving shafts of sunlight. A few gulls gathered on the point for a brief meeting, conferred, then went about their day. The rams wandered along the shore, foraging.

White wisps of cloud drifted high above the water across a sky whose intense blueness was off the colour charts and so cannot be named. If you tried to name it you would do it an injustice, so inadequate would your effort be. A heron flew gracefully through that nameless blueness, as if it were the most natural thing in the world to sail through such a sky.

A Sort of a Garden

The back orchard is a sort of a garden, in the sense that it's sort of enclosed, by the stone walls, except in the places where the sheep and deer have broken them down. In spring the deer stand on the walls to nibble the enticing tips of apple twigs and buds. In late summer and autumn they stand on the walls to reach irresistible apples hanging from a branch. The sheep sometimes climb over the walls when they come into the orchard, or leave it. They use the two entrances as well, but they don't think of stone walls as boundaries.

I do, though. The stone walls are what turn the orchard into a garden, at least in my mind. I'll admit to a romantic turn of mind when it comes to gardens, whereas the deer and sheep are entirely practical about any island space, enclosed or not. Is there something here that we can eat, they think. I have two other gardens where those particular species of animal are not welcome. But this one is different. It's a peaceable kingdom, of a sort.

When we first came here, the stone walls were not doing their job, and the back orchard had been invaded by wildness. There were actually spruce trees there (as well as everywhere), grotesque and absurd and menacing. But now they are all gone. The wild raspberries are gone, too. I love the wild raspberries, and there are some excellent patches I could tell you about, except that they are secret. But it's the contrast between inside and outside that makes a place into a garden. So: no wild raspberries inside the back orchard walls. Also no bayberry. They have plenty of their own places on the island, just like the spruce.

This rule has lately been extended to the wild pasture rose. The wild pasture rose belongs in wild pastures, or along roadsides, or hidden deep among the bayberry along the shore, where in June you can just glimpse its pink blossoms as you go by. A glimpse of it is lovely, really quite sufficient. It doesn't need to be stared at.

On the other hand, the principles on which my rule is based are not entirely consistent. The back orchard is a place where wild ferns grow up along the walls, and snakes sun on the rocks. There are wild stones embedded in the ground. They wear old coverings, of lichen or moss, that are wild, too. You can see sheep and deer droppings everywhere. In early summer there are wildflowers -- white and pink yarrow, and daisies, and clover -- though the sheep enjoy them so much that their moment of flourishing is brief. Of course the birds do not observe any boundaries. Or the bees. These are all wild, all equally at home both inside and outside the garden, like the sheep and the deer. Nevertheless, they are all very welcome inside.

Then there are the daffodils. There is an old lilac. There are the pear and apple trees. They are domestic, garden sorts of things. You understand when you look at them that effort has been made here during the past century and a half. Eventually I would like to plant more daffodils, and a drift of day lilies, since the sheep and deer ignore them both. Maybe another lilac or two. Some roses, maybe even a rambler along a part of the wall that the animals don't use.

The back orchard will never be a domesticated place, but it has its own beauty.

Goulden House, circa 1911

It is a summer day a century ago. Someone is standing in the side yard with a camera. He, or she, steps back to show the entire house in the frame, not completely successfully. This is our house now, and for the first time I am looking at it as it once was long ago. In the photograph, a woman stands in the doorway. A man stands next to her, outside. He's holding a baby. There is a clothesline strung from the breezeway out into the yard, and a bit of laundry drying there. Maybe this is a Sunday, since the man is dressed in a well-ironed shirt and trousers.

To the right of the doorway is the dairy-keeping room and the woodshed. This is a household economy that creates what it consumes: fells trees and splits logs for heat, milks its cow and churns its butter, preserves its vegetables and fruit and fish, hunts or raises and slaughters meat.

Between the camera and its subjects there is a tall flowering hedge of some sort. It's a practical way to define the space of the house, but it's also a thing of beauty. There is more than necessity in this world.

The woman and the man are likely Bertha Snow Goulden and her husband James Andrew Goulden. They married in 1906, across the harbour in Gunning Cove. She was seventeen on her wedding day, and her fisherman husband was thirty eight -- more than twice her age.

Bertha had grown up on McNutt's Island. When the census taker came around to the island in 1901 it was duly noted that Bertha was then eleven years old, the oldest of five children, and that she lived with her parents Arthur and Melinda Snow and her brothers and sisters. Her father was a fisherman, too, like nearly every man she knew.

James and Bertha bought the house in 1911 from its builder and first owner, old man William Perry. Bertha knew this house well, from her childhood. It was a part of her deeply familiar world. And she would live here, and go in and out of this door, until the last two days of her life. She died in July 1952, not at home on the island, but at Roseway Hospital across the harbour in Sandy Point.

If the picture was taken soon after the Gouldens moved into the house, then it captures Bertha in her early twenties and James in his early forties. By the time they moved across the harbour to the island she and James already had three young children. She will bear seven others in this house, and she and James will raise all of them here.

It is a photograph of an ordinary moment in an ordinary day. "I've brought my camera," the photographer announces. "Come out so I can take your picture." James doesn't mind; he seems to enjoy it, and even poses a bit. Bertha is shyer, or maybe just in the middle of doing something else. She won't come completely outside, but stands in the doorway and looks out into the summer light.

Welcome, Baby Robins

This is the second summer I've been surprised by the baby robins. It's because they are almost the same size as their mommies and daddies by the time we realize what exactly we are seeing in the back orchard or the front yard. They're speckled brown on their breasts and backs, though, and they have a certain tentative quality about them. Often you see them just standing there, looking around vacantly, waiting to be fed. They don't seem to be entirely sure what this is all about. It's endearing.

Meanwhile the parent -- mother or father, I don't know which -- is nearby, lovingly digging up worms and hopping over and direct-delivering them into the mouth of the baby who doesn't look much like a baby. The "little" one follows its parent around, and makes the most remarkable sounds, like a tiny radio on the fritz, with all kinds of random screeches and static and buzzing. When there are two or three babies in the yard all hopping desperately after their mothers or fathers and going on like that you can hardly hear yourself think.

One was making a huge racket yesterday afternoon, almost on the front porch. Its mother or father was half-way across the yard, so maybe it was feeling lost and anxious. Or maybe it was just yelling "I want my dinner!" Or "Wow, I've never seen so much grass!" Whatever it was saying, it seemed clear that basically it was pretty clueless about the world.

Goodbye, Rams

The rams were peacefully lounging about in the lower orchard this morning when Mary and Leroy came to get them. During the recent gathering and shearing they eluded the shepherds and ran off into the woods. But today they gave up with only token resistance. Now at last they'll get rid of those hot wool coats they've been wearing all summer. At the end of the day they'll be going off to Ram Island, a well-earned vacation break after all their hard work here on McNutt's. We thought about throwing a going-away party for them yesterday, but a) they hadn't yet heard they were leaving and b) we didn't think they'd really enjoy a party. They are not party types.

So instead I leaned against the cart and talked to them while they lay panting in the shade of the log palace. I told them that I hoped they would be safe and happy on Ram Island, and that I hoped they would come back here in December. I told Bertie and Balzac and The Major that they had been very kind to young Fred.

I told them that I would miss them. And I will. They are comical and lovable fellows.

Picking Peas

I pick a cup or so of sugar snap peas every morning now, and every morning the pea vines have gotten taller. Now they arch beyond the trellis, which is five feet high. To reach the highest pods tomorrow, I'll need to get on a rickety chair -- a derelict wooden one that's lost its back and is spending its last days waiting to be of some use in the garden. When I snap a pod dangling above my head, the fine early morning mist that still hangs about the vine and leaves showers down on my face, an island version of a beauty treatment.

I wasn't thinking when I decided to put the trellis along the outer edge of a bed. The peas are easy to harvest from that side, but if I want to reach the ones that hang enticingly at the centre of the trellis on the inside, and I do, I have to teeter on the wooden frame of the raised bed, stretch over two or three feet, steady myself with one hand along the trellis frame, and then try to pick each of those peas -- which are clearly the very best of the lot -- with only one hand. A weird new yoga pose. Although you really do need two hands to pick snap peas. So it's far better if you can do it while standing well-balanced on the earth on your two feet. I'd be standing on chard if I tried that. It's what you could call a design flaw.

This western side of the island has such high winds that the trellises blew over during the garden's first summer. We lost the last of the peas that year. After that Greg sank the posts into concrete to keep them upright through the whole season. So where they are is where they will be: what you could call a permanent design flaw.

But the pea trellis is not the only design flaw. Some of the raised beds are too wide. It's a big stretch to reach into the middle to cut greens or pull weeds. My early miscalculations put me in awkward positions every day.

I'm bringing all sorts of things into the house these days besides the peas: huge baskets of collards and turnip greens, chard, kale, curly lime-coloured mustard, great piles of lettuce. I can vaguely remember all the work that went into this year's garden -- the raised beds, the winter seaweed, the spring digging, the compost.

But there are essential elements that have nothing to do with either how hard I've worked or how many mistakes I've made: the balance of sun and rain, the pace at which summer has unfolded here on the island, the warmth of the season. Except for the watering, I have little power over any of that. So when I'm picking the peas or cutting the collards my basic position is amazed.

Harvesting Rockweed

Rockweed grows along the shore of the island's western cove. It's inter-tidal, so it grows on the boulders that line the cove, gripping the rocks' hard surface with its holdfasts. It lives in the sea, but then twice a day the sea ebbs away from its home. And so its environment changes, and then it lies for a while along the shore exposed to direct sunlight and air. The rising tide will lift it up and set it to swaying back and forth again for several hours.

It does well in the coves and harbours along the southwest Nova Scotia coast. Rockweed is harvested by hand, using a special rake that prunes the plant without damaging its holdfast. The harvesters stand in their wide, deep boats, cutting and lifting the rockweed in one continuous motion. It takes several hours to fill a boat. Rockweed harvesting is such a quiet activity that usually I don't even realize the boats are down in the cove unless I happen to see one, tucked along the shore.

Raymond, the harvester I met yesterday, said he would have 10,000 to 12,000 pounds in his boat by the time he had finished for the day. A boat filled with rockweed rides very low in the water and must be navigated carefully back to the dock to be unloaded. Raymond was kind enough to visit with me for a while as he filled his boat and I stood on the shore. He is from nearby, from around Barrington. He has been harvesting rockweed and Irish moss since he was fourteen years old. He goes lobstering until the end of May when the lobster season ends. After the lobster season he harvests rockweed.

"It's not hard," he told me. But it looks hard, standing in your boat, braced against the rocking of the waves, reaching down into the water and cutting the rockweed and lifting it up and flipping it from the rake into the bottom of the boat, without losing your balance, over and over and over again. It is a beautiful sight to watch, though, like something from an earlier time.

Rockweed has an intrinsic value in the marine environment, providing a refuge and a nursery for any manner of marine life. But it's also very useful in a wide array of products that are manufactured all over the world, and its harvesting is important to the economy of south western Nova Scotia. There was a time, thirty or so years ago, when some Norwegians tried to harvest rockweed in the Bay of Fundy with huge machines, with predictable results.

That technique is banned now, and people only harvest rockweed by hand, the way it's been done for generations.

Backyard Visitor

The island is veiled in fog today. In the morning a young heron, the colour of fog, stood on the back wall. Maybe he was looking around for fish. He flew off across the orchard to settle briefly in an apple tree. His vast wingspan made a poor fit with its dense branches and homely leaves. He seemed incongruous there among robins' nests, like some ancient pagan god visiting a simple peasant's hut.

Then he flew south, across the lower orchard, toward the cove. The shore is the usual feeding place of the heron, not our back yard. His visit was a reminder of how closely the familiar and the wild dwell together here. It's something I forget. Then a glimpse of that strange otherness and grace illuminates everything, and I remember again for a little while.

Apple Tree Report

We have lately noticed a single young deer wandering among the apple trees around the house. He is a yearling, recently forced away from his mother when she gave birth to this year's fawn. Now he is a bit lonely, adjusting to his suddenly grown-up place in the world.

But he does have the apples, for they have begun to drop from some of the trees. They are tiny things about one inch in diameter. The little deer is drawn here by their fragrance, and finds comfort in them. As surely as the golden birch leaves we have found along the main road, he is a sign that summer is already ripening into autumn.

The deer love the apples, and as the season turns toward fall we will spy more and more of them emerging from the forest or floating ghostly among the bayberry near the shore, standing in the lower orchard or grazing peacefully in the backyard. In the twilight we will watch the sheep and the deer eating apples together, a tableau of harmony. They fall under an enchantment of apples, and forget to be afraid.

When we first came here the apple trees were so ancient and untended, the apples so small and so unlike any apple you would ever buy in a store, and we so overwhelmed by other things, that we ignored them. Since then Greg has pruned them all and we have bought a cider press, and last fall we picked apples and pressed cider for the first time.

But we will not devote our lives to these apple trees. Greg will prune them each spring. But from here on the pruning will be nothing radical. There is a beauty, after all, in their gnarled shapes. The apples will still be only tentatively identified, at best. We have done as much as we choose to do in the way of restoring them. Now we are happy to let them be what they are.

Their old craggy bark will continue to provide insects for the birds to eat, their twisted branches places for nests. Their blossoms in spring will hum with wild bees. In winter, small animals will find safe homes in the hollow places among their roots. And for the next few months, as the island slips from summer toward winter, sheep and deer will graze among their dropped fruit.

Turning the Compost Piles

I have mostly neglected the compost piles since April, when I built a new base out of the dead ferns I raked away from the stone walls. After that I have only dumped the garbage pail and weeds from the garden, and once in a while flipped some of the bottom-dwelling stuff up to the top. The piles became unwieldy, and sometimes I saw a snake going in and out. After a while it got to the point that when I walked past them I preferred to look in some other direction.

Who knows why the snake had grown in my imagination into a writhing furious nest that would seek my harm. My imagination sometimes works that way. When I finally addressed the compost piles yesterday, the reality was modest and benign. I found one snake, a darkly glistening maritime garter. She had recently shed her old skin and left it behind on top of the heap. She was surprised to have her cover blown and immediately moved into the second pile. Later in the day she had to move again, into the third pile. This morning I will work on that pile and disturb her for a last time. She seems to take life as it comes. Probably she does not waste her time on imaginary dangers. Maybe she will move back to the first pile. If she does she will find it much improved.

At the water's edge, eelgrass lay darkly glistening in a sinuous line where the high tide had left it behind. I gathered it along with broken branches of rockweed, washed-up gleanings from the work of the rockweed harvesters. I carried big armloads of the stuff from the rocks to the cart-- some of it dried and brittle, some wet and gelatinous, huge portions of dripping black and brown noodles, containing essence of sea.

I moved each compost heap from one side of its bin to the other, lifting its material with the pitchfork and layering it with seaweed. Released to the air, it smelled good -- damp and rich, like essence of earth. I uncovered plenty of worms, who unlike the snake have no need to move anywhere. They are already completely at home in an artisanal mix of decomposing ferns, woodstove ash, eggshells, tea bags, potato peelings, apple cores, pea vines, dock, clover, eelgrass, rockweed, and bits of sea sponge with a dash of snakeskin.

The task I dreaded turned out to be nothing but pleasure, intensely absorbing, more like play than work. Turning the compost piles revealed an entrance into another of the hidden dimensions that lie everywhere here, waiting to be noticed. I have apprenticed myself to the worms and am now a devoted novice brewer of planetary essences: earth, sea, fog, tide, sun, rain, time.

Quiet Time for Birds

The song birds are quiet these days. Once in a while, during the day, a thin and sketchy version of the white-throated sparrow's song floats across the air. Its volume has been turned down, and the song stops and begins again at random. It is as if a bored deejay is idly lifting the needle from a spinning record and replacing it further down the groove. The summer dance party is winding down. The white-throated sparrow does not need to announce his presence or defend his tree any longer. His babies have hatched and passed the first dangerous hurdles of life -- crows, gulls, et cetera -- or not. But in any event he is preparing to move on, which does not require much in the way of singing.

The matter of babies can be confusing for somebody like me who does not know what to look for. By the time the young are out and about they are nearly as big as their parents. The other day I watched a yard full of robins searching for insects and worms. Looking, I realized that it was a sight I had not seen for some time. The robins had disappeared in June, when they were nesting. Except for that hyper vigilant mother who guarded the nest in the grape arbour and loudly scolded me every time I came into the garden. Now I saw that many of the dozen or so robins in the yard had the speckled breasts of juveniles, though they all seemed pretty much the same size. If I had not looked at them more carefully I would not have known I was seeing babies.

It was the same with the great blue herons. For a couple of weeks the sky seemed filled with them, flying back and forth in their diagonal flight pattern from the eastern side of the island toward the cove. I did not understand what I was seeing. Where did they all come from? I wondered then. It did not occur to me that the babies would by then be as big as their parents, even though I had seen that one tentative young heron in the backyard, enormous and gawky. Then the sky emptied of herons and they were gone.

This silence and emptiness will continue to settle slowly on the island over the next month or so. It's a *via negativa* that gives clarity to the summer's jumbled intensity, like a developing photograph emerges from the emulsion bath of the darkroom. But secretive little birds will continue to flit silently through the spruce forests, and many of the robins will remain over the winter, along with the gulls and the crows, who will party on.

At the Corner of Barnyard & Wild

Our shepherd friends would be leaving Nova Scotia for three weeks to work at a sheep dog competition in Ontario. Since we were intrigued by the idea of keeping goats and chickens, but intimidated by our complete lack of experience, they proposed that we keep theirs while they were away. "You'll see how easy it is," they assured us. Thus do Mary and Leroy lure us deeper into adventure. So one day they arrived on the island in their lobster boat, *Wistan Cap*, and unloaded three goats, ten hens and a rooster, along with all their gear: an instant barnyard.

The gear included a portable electric fence, for keeping the goats where we wanted them to stay. If they touched the wires they would get a mild shock, enough to remind them to stay inside its boundary. Otherwise they would be likely to barge through the perimeter, which was really just a few wires strung between plastic poles, and wander off. We set up the fence and Leroy made sure it was working before he and Mary left.

Early the next morning, for some reason, I walked the perimeter of the fence. I found first one, then another, and another huge toad lying dead along the fence line. There were four toads all together -- grandfather toads, by the size of them: venerable, and even in death embodying the great dignity of their kind. The last toad I found was still breathing. I bent down and looked as closely at him as I could. His breath came slowly, at intervals, and I could see his sides moving with the effort. His skin was dry, delicate, mottled with subtle colours. He was beautiful, and he broke my heart.

The toads had, I guess, done what they had been doing on every warm night of their lives, which was to travel slowly along some trail known only to toads, back and forth from the bog that lay below the house. Up until this particular summer night, in the whole history of island toads, an electric fence had never once interrupted their path. They hadn't known to expect it. Encountering a new obstacle, they had tried to lumber over the bottom strand of fence wire and the shock had killed them.

I felt shocked myself, and grieved and helpless, and guilt-stricken, too. "I didn't know!" I wanted to say to the toads, as if they cared about my role in their deaths. I knew now that I should have kept a vigil on the first night of the electric fence. I should have protected the toads. Now I craved their forgiveness, but they had travelled on, beyond me, and it was not within their power to offer it anyway. Forgive us our trespasses, the ancient prayer goes, but just because I wanted to be forgiven doesn't mean I am, especially by toads. Maybe I'll just have to live with that.

There are untold invisible pathways that criss-cross the island and the sky above it and the sea around it, an intricate web of complexity that I barely know of. After three years of living here I had thought I was becoming more watchful. But now the island was introducing other, deeper lessons.

I could only see bits and pieces of the whole of this small place, which can, in the blink of an eye, become vast. I could not keep from getting entangled as my own haphazard journey crossed the island's connective skein. I could not walk sure-footed on my own through a secret landscape, the one that lay beyond the apparent. I needed mercy at every step. And the best I could do was to pay attention, however awkwardly, even to what was unknowable; to try at least to look into the shimmering pied beauty of the world around me, though I would never see its glory whole, and to keep a safe place in my heart for the toad.

First Day with Chickens and Goats

In the morning I heard the first crow of the rooster at about 5:15. What an excellent sound. Chevron is very good at crowing. Unlike some roosters I have known, he did not crow all night long, expecting the sun to come up early as a result. He knows that the world does not spin at his beck and call. Instead, he crowed as the sky was beginning to lighten. He is that rare thing, a modest rooster, but diligent in his responsibilities.

I lay in bed and rehearsed my own new responsibilities. I wished they were as familiar to me as Chevron's are to him. But I told myself I would just have to bumble and stumble my way through them a few times and they would become easier. I got up and got the right amount of feed for Molly out of the shed, then a warm, damp cloth and the milk pail, and I was ready to go with my first ever milking. It is a lovely thing to be on the cusp of a new life experience.

Molly came from the shed willingly not out of any affection for me -- we are barely acquaintances yet -- but because of the feed I put in the trough of her milking stand. After she got herself on the platform I closed the wooden bars that keep her head forward and felt quite proud of myself. I washed her teats and udder with the warm damp cloth and felt that everything was going smoothly.

Then I started milking. But nothing came out. Not even a first tiny drop. Her teats seemed full but then they deflated like little balloons when I tried to get a stream of milk. I must have been using my fingers all wrong, even though it seemed so easy when we were watching Mary yesterday and trying it ourselves. Now I could tell that Molly knew I was no Mary. After much futile effort I decided to ask for a second opinion. But Greg couldn't get a thing going, either. Meanwhile Molly, who is known for her placid nature, had become a bit annoyed with our awkward attempts. It is a humbling thing to be in the midst of a new life experience.

So we let her off the milking stand and eventually her kid, Heidi, began nursing. Heidi is the designated back-up plan for milking. She's as good at nursing as Chevron is at crowing. And I, a stranger who peers longingly over the farm fence, will try to breach that border again tomorrow.

Adventures in Milking

Greg and I are alternating the milking duties so that we each can learn how to do it. So every other day I lie cozily in bed while Greg stumbles out into the misty dawn with his milking pail in hand. And then, vice versa. It's August, the days have been clear so far, it's the best of all possible worlds for milking a goat in the early hours of the day.

So, let's see. The first day I milked, I got nada. Both Molly's owner Mary and Elaine, a reader who has kept goats, told me to nudge her hard with my hand, like a kid bumping up against her stomach and udder. That worked. So then the second day I was doing pretty well until Molly knocked over the pail. I kept milking just to get her milked, but it was strictly a practice session after that. The third day, I got my full complement of three and a half cups.

So I approached my duties this morning with some degree of confidence. I was getting better every day. But the learning curve is seldom smooth. I had almost finished when Molly somehow performed a Houdini-like move and escaped from the milking stand. O magical goat! Perhaps tomorrow she will begin to float about in the sky, like one of those goats in a Chagall painting.

But I was able to grab the pail and save the milk. She and I were both contending with mosquitoes who were taking advantage of our captive positions. I had decided to just endure them, but Molly was more stubbornly opposed. More goat-like, come to think of it. Next time I will make sure the latch on top of the milking stand is properly fastened before I start. There are several small things to remember when milking a goat, and they are all of equal importance.

The Happiness of Chickens

Once upon a time in Delaware, far inland from its beautiful beaches and busy summer resort life, I came to a stop behind a huge transport truck filled with chickens. They were on their way to one of the massive poultry factories that rise from that flat landscape like castles lording it over their fiefdom. There were hundreds -- maybe even thousands -- of chickens on that truck. They sat squeezed into cages, unable to stand or move. All they could do was look out.

Being around the sheep has taught me that animals do have emotional lives, no matter what anyone says. But even back then, when I knew nothing, really, about animals, I could see that those chickens were sad. You could actually see a cloud of sadness hanging all over that truck. Probably the driver was sad, and the poultry factory workers. And maybe later on the grocers became sad, and the stock boy replenishing the frozen chicken section in the Safeway, and the people who bought them and took them home and cooked them and ate them were touched by sadness, too, without knowing why.

I remember those sad chickens because our visiting chickens are so contented. All day long they walk where they want to walk, and wriggle about in dusty places, and sit under the shade, and eat bugs and anything else they see that looks good -- and there's a lot that does look good to these chickens. They find cool shady places to sit. They drink water when they're thirsty, and they cluck to each other and do whatever Chevron the rooster says when they feel like it and ignore him when they want to. They lay eggs every day, and as evening falls they make their way up the steps into the roost and settle down for the night, always under Chevron's watchful eye.

It's plain to see that they demonstrate a certain chickenly happiness. I suppose it would be too complicated and difficult to change the world so that all chickens could have at least a taste of this sort of life. It wouldn't only benefit the chickens. I can attest that their happiness spreads to anyone who is lucky enough to watch them as they go about their daily rounds. Every time I catch sight of them they make me smile.

Being at Home in the World

I go out in my rowboat only when the water is calm, so there's no need to row to actually get somewhere, or to keep myself from being taken away from where I want to go. And besides, wherever I am in that boat is pretty much where I want to be. Any destination is fine, and sort of made up at the last minute, and bound to change again a few minutes after that. So I zig and zag and stop and start, not doing much and not going anywhere in particular.

Instead, I ship my oars and lean over the edge of the boat to watch the bottom of the harbour. I drift on the current while images stream past below me: rocks flecked with light and limpets or hidden beneath tangled golden piles of waving rockweed, schools of tiny silvery fish, white sand, underwater fields of bright green sea grass, whelks, clamshells, a lone laggardly jellyfish, and huge scary fingers of kelp like a monstrous bronze hand reaching out to grab the boat from below and drag it down to a watery grave. I'm away from each sight as soon as I arrive.

In particular places beneath the water, as if cast upon a soft bed of pale sand, I began to notice what appeared to be perfectly round and flat black objects. As I looked more closely I could see that these dark round objects bore the sand dollar's five petal pattern, but in reverse, like a wax resist technique using fine sand instead of wax to reveal the pattern. The sand dollar is an ocean filter, sucking in organic matter beneath it and releasing water through the tiny holes that form its petal pattern on top. What I could see was, I think, the residue of its filtering process.

Even at low tide they lie a couple of meters below the surface, beyond my reach. That's just as well. As it is I can only look but not touch, as if I am visiting a collection of rare masterpieces. I doubt they are rare. But who knows anymore what's rare or endangered? Things seem to slip away without our noticing, and then they are gone. For now these sand dollars remain where they belong, on the ocean floor, their dignity intact, doing whatever small obscure thing it is they do on behalf of the world.

Humming Garden

There's not much reason to spend time in the garden these days but I do it anyway. Oh, I'm harvesting peas and bush beans and lettuce, collards and turnip greens and Swiss chard and mustard greens. But mostly I'm just looking at things grow: squash, tomatoes, peppers, eggplant, cucumbers, pole beans. It gives me an excuse to wander around surrounded by the sound of a hundred bees humming away. They've been hard at work in the garden all summer long. Just because the season is turning slowly toward fall is no reason to change their ways as far as they are concerned. They are utterly and completely devoted to their purpose, like tiny levitating mantra-chanting monks.

When we first moved to the island we couldn't imagine how anything got pollinated, since there were no honey bees. We've learned that's one thing we can cross off our worry list. The wild bees take care of everything. They don't make honey so humans don't think they are just the end-all and be-all. But humans can be short-sighted that way.

I have read that the wild bees are mostly solitary (except for the bumble bees), and live in narrow bee-sized hiding places in old wood, and in the earth. In the fall the adults lay their eggs in these hiding places and seal them over, then die. In spring the eggs hatch out and the next generation emerges. So wherever you walk around our house you may be walking over, or past, the hiding places of bees, and not even have the slightest idea of it.

Days of Grace

Nova Scotians would have a few days of grace before the hurricane's arrival, the province's weather forecaster said earlier this week.

One night Greg made a list of everything we needed to do before the storm. He has been crossing items off the list since then. This morning he went into town, while the harbour is still calm. When he comes home we will intensify our preparations to secure everything.

But some things can't be secured. There's the oak tree just in front of the house. Myrtle Goulden, who was born in this house and grew up here, told us that her brother Burns planted that tree as a gift to his mother. Bertha had wanted an oak tree. He may have planted an acorn, or maybe a sapling. Myrtle wasn't sure which. Burns was born in this house in 1914 and Myrtle said he planted the tree when he was about twelve. So it's around eighty years old now. It's the only oak tree on McNutt's.

The tree is very close to the house. Over the years it has been pruned so that its branches do not actually hang above the roof. But still, it is very close. In summer it harbours the birds and gives us shade. In autumn it protects us from the westerly winds. In winter its bare branches give us beauty. It is home to lichen and mosses. And this time of year it is full of leaves and wind resistance. It could blow over in the coming storm.

These days of grace have given us time to prepare. But they also give us a chance to touch the oak tree's branches, to admire the curve of its wide embrace. For all that we can't make secure, we can somehow tell our gratitude now, just in case.

Sheep Savers, a love story

"There's a good mother," Greg said. The ewe had positioned herself on a rock in the yard, the better to face in the direction of her distant lamb. We could hear the lamb's answering cry each time the ewe bleated, which was constantly. We thought the lamb was down at the fish house. They were calling back and forth, so we thought a reunion would be happening soon. It didn't seem like anything extraordinary.

I went on down to the dock to bail out my rowboat, *Roseneath*. She had taken a lot of water in the latest rainstorm and it was past time for me to dry her out. As I approached the dock I could hear the lamb more clearly. It wasn't at the fish house after all. At first I thought it might be caught somewhere near the dock, but soon I realized that it was way over on the point, the shingle beach that is the cove's southern arm. Now I could see it wandering disconsolately back and forth, answering its mother. The point is a long way around the cove from the fish house and I wondered how they would find each other.

I watched a skiff coming across the channel from the direction of Gunning Cove. It went on around the outside of the point, in the direction of the lighthouse. The lamb and the ewe continued calling to each other across the cove. By now the ewe and a couple of her ewe friends had walked further down the path to the fish house. She was standing on the shore, looking out over the water in the direction of the point, still calling to her lamb.

Sometime later I began to hear the lamb making a different sound. Written on the page, it could look like: glub, glub, baaa -- glub, glub, baaa. The baaas were growing weaker, too. In its determination to find its mother, the lamb had decided to take the shortest route. It had plunged into the cove waters and was trying to swim across. It would never make it, though. The waters were placid but the distance from shore to shore is about two hundred yards. It would tire and drown.

Then I heard the skiff coming slowly into the cove. Evidently the boaters -- an older man, a younger man, and a couple of kids and dogs -- had noticed the lamb on their way out, then seen it in the water as they were coming back. They had decided to help. They cut the motor and rowed toward the lamb. I had climbed up onto our dock, and watched one of them reach over the side of the boat and hold the lamb's head as they slowly motored across the cove, toward the fish house. I heard one of them say, "I can't believe we are sheep savers!"

When they approached the fish house and the rocky shore there, they let the lamb go. But instead of heading toward the shore, it swam in a circle around the boat and tried to stay with it. Then the boaters held its head again and using their oars they rowed among the underwater rocks, closer to the shore. They let the lamb go again and this time it swam to shore and slowly clambered up rockweed-covered rocks.

All this time the mother had been watching, standing next to the fish house. Now she began calling out again. I thought the lamb would be exhausted but since it had a free ride, it wasn't. It trotted through the woods and met up with its mother and her two ewe friends. There was much wiggling and greeting and then the four of them pranced merrily up the path together. The sheep savers went on their way, having done a very good deed which I was lucky to observe.

I had bailed out *Roseneath* by now, so I rowed out to check the gill net. When I came back the little group had moved into the lower orchard. The lamb looked especially clean after its bath in the cove, and it was keeping close to its mother.

Welcome to Bean World

The beans are flourishing, and I am beginning to think maybe I planted too many of them. There are two trellises of pole beans and two beds of bush beans. The bush bean seed packet contained a few random pole beans put there by some trickster seed packet packer somewhere, so there are also pole beans sprawling around among their more upright and conscientious relatives and making awkward late night take-over moves, ambitious climbers with no place to go. Meanwhile, in the actual designated pole bean bed, the horizontal cross bar on one of the trellises -- an eight foot long 2"x 2" milled from island spruce -- sagged and sagged until at last it snapped in half under the weighty morass of twisted vines, spreading leaves and dangling beans. I don't care, though.

Every other morning I work my way around this trellis, parting a dense jungle of leaves and dodging bees to peer as deeply into bean world as I dare. The challenge is making sense of such manic, burgeoning complexity. I can only see parts of beans amid fractured shards of shadow and sunlight. They are rarely dangling properly as they are supposed to, more often wedged up behind the trellis netting or lolling across a twisted bunch of leaves. Some of them do hide in plain sight, growing larger and larger until even the most distracted seeker could find them, gigantic foot-long beans, cartoon beans, beans guaranteed to get your attention no matter what.

I begin my every-other morning bean harvest with a slow, patient, systematic search for normal-size beans. Be mindful, I tell myself. Be Zen-like. Appreciate the beans. Let the beans be your teacher. But pretty soon my disciplined approach breaks down into something primitive, *Lord of the Flies*-ish. Even though it's early, the garden is hot, and there are mosquitoes about, and my hands have a mind of their own. Half way around the trellis they assert themselves, not at all mindfully. Whatever they locate by accident, they take. Whatever they miss, they miss and don't even know it. My hands are in a hurry, and greedy. They are focused on the bottom line. So many beans! they think. Let's get this over with. My hands get impatient and they don't look back.

Later we eat a few of these many, many beans, which Greg has sautéed in olive oil with garlic and tomatoes. Briefly, I manage to allow a tiny sliver of amazement. What we are eating here -- what is giving us sustenance and keeping us from hunger -- these green beans, our daily bread -- came directly into our kitchen and thence onto our supper plates from the combination of seeds and dirt and sun and water and season: a miraculous harvest, even if there's a part of me that takes it for granted every single time.

The Names of Things

You lack the names of things when you go to a new place. I have been like a toddler the past two years, asking over and over, what's that? Or like a sneaky toddler, not asking outright but listening hard to add to my store of island words.

There is a word that Robin taught me the first summer we were on the island. The tufts of wool that are caught in the branches when the sheep brush against them on their endless circuit around the island: rovings. Rovings are not just useless remnants hanging randomly on island brambles, like you might think. There's a great deal you can do with rovings. You can collect them, which would be wool-gathering. You can card, spin, weave or knit them, or if you are lazy and skill-less like me and not actually needing to make clothes since there is such a thing as Nova Scotia's amazing used clothes store, Frenchy's, you could just put the rovings in a basket and look at them fondly now and then.

We inherited many amazing and wonderful things with our island house: three chipped and crazed china plates with rabbits running in an endless circle around the edge; a daguerreotype of two young women; an ancient padlock. But of all the treasures we inherited, the very most wonderful is an anchor made of wood and weighted with a stone. And this kind of old home-made anchor is called a killick. Peter gave us this word.

The standing dead trees we see everywhere are called snags. This is a word I found by reading an essay called Ode to Dead Wood, from The Canadian Wildlife Federation website. Here you can learn just how valuable our snags are -- and we have so many! Like rovings, snag is a word that fits snugly with the object itself.

Then there are the fragrant white flowers that bloom all around the house in early summer. I thought they were narcissus, but Skipper called them June lilies, a more apt name for them. Lucy Maude Montgomery writes about June lilies on Prince Edward Island, so maybe they are June lilies throughout the Maritime provinces.

Another name I learned from Skipper was conspicuous boulder. It's a navigational term that refers to, well, conspicuous boulders, like the huge ice-age rock that teeters at Fort Point, or like The Sloop, which is the name of the conspicuous sloop-like boulder that defines the southwest corner of McNutt's.

Wherever we go, necessary and useful words are waiting there for us. So vast is our ignorance that we don't even know they exist until we need them. Then they come out of nowhere, where they have been waiting, and light on our palms like butterflies, slowly opening and closing their wings.

The Magicians

I climb out of my rowboat onto the dock and stare down into the water. From this perspective I can see that I have been rowing --all unknowing -- through swarming schools of tiny fish. As far as I know they don't have a name. When I asked around, people said they were just the little fish that bigger fish like to eat.

Now they turn and wheel in synchrony, quick and flowing at the same time. Their bodies flash silver as sunlight penetrates the water. But it's only for an instant, like a strobe light. The effect is of hundreds of flashing, gleaming silver shards blinking off and on as light sinks below dark rippling water. Though they appear to be, the fish are not tumbling about randomly. They are schooling in perfect formation. It's the light on their bodies that plays a trick on my eyes.

By the time I have tied the rowboat's painter to the dock and turned back to look again, they are gone without a trace. It's as if they were never there at all.

I begin my walk back to the house from the dock. It is a slow walk. An observer might think I am practicing walking meditation, I go so slowly. Instead I'm watching the warblers as they dart and flash through the bayberry bushes that line the shore and dominate the bog below the house.

I used to fret about these bushes and consult my reference books, back when I thought I could learn the names of everything. They seemed bayberry-ish, but lacked that essential element, berries. Now I see that the tiny waxy berries disappear down tiny warbler gullets and into tiny warbler bellies. They will pick these bayberry bushes nearly clean, carbo-loading for their upcoming marathon.

They are masters of the now-you-see-it-now-you-don't-school of performance art. They hide, and flit, and dart, and there are so many different varieties of them. I stare and stare, trying to distinguish the different warblers that the birding lists tell me come through here on their way south for the winter: Palm, Black and White, Common Yellow Throat, Northern Parula, so many others.

But they are too quick for me. Their colours are various, too, and subtle: now and then there's an Impressionist's brushstroke of cream, a flash of yellow, a gleam of gold. For a moment I am able to let go of my need to know their names. When I look at them from this perspective they are magical.

Season of Harvest and Loss

Introduction: Unmetaphorical Harvest

I thought I knew something about harvest before we moved to the island, because I was familiar with biblical images and scenes from literature and art and the old harvest hymns. They were powerful images but tinted by nostalgia, since they evoked a world that didn't seem to exist anymore, at least not as far as I could see from where I stood.

Back then there was nothing of seasons to the food I ate. I could buy any kind of food I wanted, all year around. Innocent, sort of, I dwelled back then in a kind of enchanted Eden, brought to me by a vast unseen network finally made visible in a pile of gleaming green Granny Smith apples at my local Safeway. Somebody somewhere sometime had harvested those apples but it sure wasn't me.

Now, like so much else, harvest was becoming less metaphorical, more grounded. I had never imagined all the steps in harvesting something. Once you'd gone to all the work of growing it, you still couldn't just pick it and bring it into the house. That was usually only the start of some other intricate and heretofore unfamiliar process: blanching and freezing, or cooking, straining and canning, or peeling, or drying.

And while we tried to figure out how to do whatever needed to be done next, those harvested vegetables lying in great heaps in the kitchen — taking up table surfaces, and chairs, and floor space, using up every available basket, bowl, box and pot -- were still going on about their business of ripening or rotting or shrivelling up. They operated on their own schedule and weren't waiting around for us to get with the program. Up until I picked them the collards and Swiss chard and beans were the most unassuming of plants, asking nothing much of me all through their growing season. But the minute I picked them they became quite demanding. So for a while in the fall, the world revolves around what's coming out of the garden.

Timing mattered for other kinds of harvests, too. One year, by accident, we foraged for cranberries on the perfect day. But the next year I dillied and dallied while some other foragers — the birds and the deer, most likely — beat me to the crop. I was too late and that year we got no wild cranberries.

Autumn brings fullness and abundance; but there is loss, too. Birds waft away overnight, angling south. After they have gleaned our windfall apples, the deer disappear into the forest. The shepherds come for the lambs. One day you realize you haven't seen a snake in a long time, for all unbeknownst they have crept into their secret places and closed their eyes. And so even though (of course, being so wrapped up in the harvest and all) you missed the exact, precious moment of it, still, now you stop whatever you are doing and whisper a little blessing to the snakes: sweet dreams.

How the Music Changes

The birds have been slipping away for some time now. I last saw the hummingbirds one evening a week or so ago, so I guess they left that night or early the next morning. They didn't say good-bye, even after we had such a good time together. The juncos and sparrows and mourning doves have left too, along with their babies. The woods where the kinglets dwell are silent. And I haven't seen the robins for a while, though some of them winter over here, so maybe they are only taking a short vacation.

Yesterday I heard a white-throated sparrow's half-hearted song, and there's still one small sparrow of some sort who believes the vegetable garden is her personal kingdom. Other than those laggards, most of the beautiful singers -- the ones that make you stop whatever you're doing and listen -- have gone away and they didn't say where.

As sometimes happens, when the lead singers go off in search of greater glory or at least someplace warmer, you are not exactly bereft after all. It turns out that there were other musicians here all along, practicing quietly to themselves and waiting for their moment. Now their moment has come and they are ready. Bees and grasshoppers and dragonflies saw away on their tiny fiddles. Red squirrels add percussive texture. Lamb and ewe duets offer heart-felt recitative. The seal chorus really only knows its one song, but they love it dearly and never get tired of singing it over and over, their end-of-summer lament.

And there's the single loon who lives year-round in the cove. She's an aged alto, once famous but now retired to this obscure spot. She's still got her voice, and when she sings the island's enthusiastic amateurs fall silent, as anybody would in the presence of greatness.

Golden Day

It is an almost unbearably beautiful day on the island. The light is golden, and everything -- apples, sheep, stones, deer, water -- is shining with it. The oak tree and the bayberry bog are filled with tiny warblers and you can catch just a glimpse of golden feathers when they spread their wings. Boats come and go into the cove, filled with visitors and guests for the long weekend. The teenagers have brought their ATVs, and they ride back and forth along the road, traveling between the camps looking for fun, which may be over at the other camp. All afternoon and late into the night they will continue to ride, back and forth. Still the golden light hovers over the island, blessing everything and all of us alike.

A Secret Place

Just as we were about to begin gathering the sheep last week, my young friend Blake said to me, "Do you want a picture of some snake eggs for your blog?" So he and Anna and I made a quick detour to a place that Blake knows about. He raised up a board and we saw six white snake eggs, oblong in shape and about three centimeters long, in the cool protected dirt beneath. We did not see their mother. I took a picture and then Blake put the board back in place and we left. They are the eggs of a smooth green snake, one of the two kinds of snakes on the island. The other kind, the maritime garter snake, gives live birth to her babies.

I asked Blake how he knew the eggs would be there. He told us that the mother lays her eggs in the same spot every year. Imagine knowing something as secret as that.

Northern Pitcher Plant

The northern pitcher plant is common in Nova Scotia, where it makes its home in acidic bogs. We had not seen them here, though, until recently, when we came upon an open acidic bog on the southern end of the island. During the 1940s, when Fort McNutt and its guns were in place, much of this area was deforested. There used to be a pond here, according to those who know. Now it is an open bog -- a place where it really isn't possible to walk because you can't tell whether there is any solid ground below your feet.

The leaves of the pitcher plant are carnivorous. They emit an odour of decay that attracts insects. Then an inner lining of stiff downward-pointing hairs sends the insects sliding into small pools of water that collect in the base of the leaves. There dreadful things happen to them, but quickly, before they know it.

Meanwhile the pitcher plant's blood-red flower rises serenely above the carnage. In an acidic bog there is little nitrogen available for the roots of plants. The decomposed insects become usable nitrogen for this graceful flower.

An open bog is a phase in a process. Eventually the bog will dry out as it fills in with layer upon layer of decomposing mosses and grasses and other plant life. The mosses will become peat, and the spruces that now surround the bog will invade it. It will become a forest again, and the pitcher plant will not grow here any longer.

Our Daily Bread

When we arrived on the island in the spring of 2007 our food situation was a little strange. We were restoring the old house, and so everything was in a kerfuffle, as they say. We got our drinking water from a good well on the other side of the island. Greg would trundle a couple of miles along a rocky path with a five gallon water jug in a wheelbarrow, fill up the jug from the well, then trundle it home again. We had no refrigerator, since we quickly disposed of the ancient kerosene refrigerator that was here when we arrived. Our cooking was on an old Coleman camp stove that we inherited with the house. We had a table set up in one little room off the kitchen. All our food was crowded onto that table: cans of things, mostly, and boxes of things you dump into boiling water, and crackers and peanut butter and cheese and store-bought cookies. It was eternal-shelf-life type food. In those days our standards were what they needed to be.

By late summer, though, we had our propane gas range hooked up, and our refrigerator and our freezer plugged in. We had cold running water, delivered via a pipe in the ground from our very own well. The house had leapt across the centuries in just a few months. But our initial experience helped me appreciate how hard it must have been to keep food safely and to make meals here in the days before electricity and running water and gas ranges.

As soon as we got the gas stove hooked up I went back to making bread. Greg is the cook around here, but I do like to make bread so I kind of hold the line there. I hadn't made bread for years, but at one time it was a regular part of my life. It took a few weeks to get into the rhythm of it again. But now we just don't ever buy bread.

Garden of Inductive Reasoning

My wildflower garden experiment so far has led me to conclude that yarrow, mallow and ox-eye daisies are all greatly enjoyed by sheep. Safe within the fence, where the sheep can't reach them, they have all grown into lovely plants. But out around the island, where they grow in the old fields and along the roads and where the sheep can eat their fill, the same flowers make a meagre showing.

Now I can add another flower to the list. Last fall I dug up a few spindly, pitiful little asters and planted them in the wildflower garden. When you see them around the island they look like something that's hiding out, aiming for inconspicuousness. It didn't seem like they had it in them to do very well in the garden, but I thought I'd give it a try.

Inside the garden, the stems and leaves began to come up in early summer. They were growing into plants so tall and graceful, so beautiful, really, that I wasn't sure it could be the same thing I had planted in those spots last fall. Maybe something else had blown in instead. Day after day I looked at them wonderingly.

I noticed that some of the stems and leaves were chewed off on the side of the plant nearest the fence. Later I caught sheep lolling about just outside the fence with their hands in their pockets, whistling innocently. And then one morning I shooed three lambs away as they shoved their muzzles between the pickets to get a taste.

According to this scientific experiment, sheep love asters. I'm happy for them to have all the asters they can eat, everywhere else on the island. But not these.

Shuttle in the Wall

Sometime in the 1850s a fisherman built this house we live in, on McNutt's Island off the south western coast of Nova Scotia. Only four families lived here over the next hundred and sixty years or so, and the house pretty much stayed the same all that time. The living room walls were old plaster, but during our first summer here we broke up the plaster and pulled out the lath. Then we insulated and wired before we finished the walls again.

When we tore out the plaster, we found a wooden shuttle hidden inside the wall directly above the front door. It has the initials M.P. carved on it, so it must have belonged to Martha Perry, whose husband Jonathan and son William built the house. Since the shuttle was inside the wall, it would have been forgotten after a while. And then after that nobody even knew it was there, until we found it.

But long ago, in an ordinary act of daily life, a weaver sat at her loom and sent this very shuttle back and forth, weaving the horizontal weft threads through the vertical warp. And so the hidden shuttle could have been Martha Perry's way of bestowing a secret blessing on all who would pass through the front door. Maybe she hoped, as she tucked the shuttle inside the lath, that the lives threading in and out of this house over the decades would be somehow woven together.

And it does seem that our lives have begun to weave into the lives of those who lived here before us: the long-ago toddler who died of scarlet fever in this house, and the young bride and her fisherman groom who were married near the door, and the boy who planted an oak tree for his mother in the front yard, and the woman who found a hard-fought peace here, whose ashes are spread in the apple grove.

After we painted the living room we returned the shuttle to its place above the door. But now it hangs on the wall, a visible reminder that everything is connected, woven together: blessed, whether we know it or not.

Remembering a Hummingbird

This place where we live is a small patch that for a couple of centuries now people have been making into their own. Its house, stone walls, crumbled cellars, apple trees, wells and old fields are evidence of the long-ago work of domesticating a bit of acreage on an island filled with bogs and rocks and forest and surrounded by the sea. It's a project we embrace, most days.

But around and beneath and above and even within this place lies another, vaster place, which is wildness. The two places live side by side and intermingled. Sometimes that other country, that wild place, is distant and impossible to discover, and sometimes it is very near. Sometimes it encroaches. Sometimes it brushes by, lighter than a feather.

This summer we hung up a hummingbird feeder for the first time. We delighted all summer in watching the frequent visits of two female hummingbirds to the feeder -- so frequent that, if you just stood for a few minutes at the front door, you would see them there, all day, every day, without fail. Because they became so familiar I thought I was getting to know them pretty well.

But then, as summer was coming to an end, I met a young hummingbird up in the vegetable garden. At first, when I saw him sitting so still for several minutes at a time, I didn't have enough to go on. It didn't fit with what I had seen near the feeder. So I thought he might be sick or dying. Why was he allowing me to get so close? I began to spin a sort of hummingbird tragedy in my mind: the little bird, somehow left behind or blown off course as his relatives all flew away across the Gulf of Maine, now lonely and afraid and stranded in the vegetable garden. It's a pretty good story, and it could be true.

Or not. It could be that he was merely on his way, alone or more or less along with others, and had stopped to rest for a few hours before moving on. The day I saw him was both sunny and windy, not a good day for flying east against a strong westerly wind, but not a bad day for being close to the ground in a relatively protected sunny garden. It's possible that he was feeling perfectly confident and able to take care of himself, within the limits of being a very small bird with a great distance yet to travel. I did not need to invent pathos where none was required, there being a big enough supply of tragedy in the world already.

Until my tutorial in the vegetable garden, I had not known that hummingbirds sit for long periods of time, stalk their prey, blink, swallow, and unroll their amazing tongues, a skill I associated only with frogs and snakes. He was, though young, an excellent teacher.

But I still don't understand what I saw that day: where he came from and where he was going and why he had come to the garden. I expect there are interpretations that I even don't know enough to consider. I only know that for an hour he became a small portal into the vast wildness that surrounds us.

Purloined Lace

I've never seen Queen Anne's Lace here on the island, even though it grows all along the roadsides just across the harbour. So when we visited *Le Village historique acadien* in Lower West Pubnico late last summer I took a dried flower head out of the garden there and shoved it into my pocket. All afternoon I felt the dry crumbly texture of the seed pod coming apart every time I touched it, hidden in its secret place. By behaving in a nonchalant manner I got away from there without being apprehended. It was about the same time that I was starting the little wildflower garden next to the house. I came home and planted the stolen seeds there.

There's no evidence for it, but some people think Acadians may have lived on this island in the seventeenth century, or at least may have used its rocky shores for drying fish. More certainly they were across the harbour to the west. So -- even though it's a wildflower that will grow just about anywhere, and does -- the Queen Anne's Lace that's growing in the garden reminds me of the ghostly presence of Acadians along south shore Nova Scotia.

Unexpected Harvest

We arrived home from a few days' absence to discover that the garden fence had been broken through and the deer and the sheep had helped themselves to just about everything. It was no use trying to figure out who the first culprit was. The garden had quickly become a well-known party destination. The sheep and the deer did not need Twitter to learn about the latest happening place. Some irresistible force drew them -- the fragrance of cabbage leaves released into the air? the faintest wafting of tomatoes? -- and they came streaming and leaping, essence of wildness, from the rocky lighthouse shore and the deep forest recesses.

Deer poured gracefully through the ragged new doorways that blossomed everywhere along the net. The sheep, less graceful but still enthusiastic, somehow manoeuvred their bodies inside too. I would have liked to have watched their silvery entrances and their moon-lit party. They were not being vandals, after all. From their point of view it had nothing to do with us. They were being wild things. I imagine them feasting inside the broken walls, a luminous medieval altar piece come to life. If there exists a Church of the Wild Things -- which there probably is, all around us, even though we have not yet noticed it -- this could be its image of the abundant love of God.

But I had a point of view, too. I was sad to lose so much: cabbage and squash, cucumbers and zucchini, peppers, tomatoes, beans, chard, mustard, mesclun. The first day I stayed away from the garden, a bit stunned. The next morning I found a couple of sheep wandering about inside it, casually exiting as they watched me approach. That day I mended the holes, using twine to draw the netting back together. It wouldn't be strong enough anymore, now that the animals had tasted paradise. But maybe it would keep them out until we could put up something better. There were still things to protect inside the garden: parsnips and leeks and potatoes and asparagus. The things they spurned.

Later Skipper brought over a bright orange flounder net. Its nylon roping is heavier than the herring net we used for the first layer. The fence will have layers, now, of teal and orange. If such a thing is possible, it will be even more beautiful than before.

On Sunday Mary and Leroy tied their skiff to the dock and walked up the hill with bags and bags of vegetables from their garden in Pubnico: zucchini, at least twenty cabbages, a huge sack of glowing red tomatoes, dozens of peppers, squash. We had asked if we could trade vegetables for the meals Greg will make the shepherds when they are here to gather and harvest the sheep later this week. But they just gave it all to us. "I wasn't going to have time to process it all anyway," Mary told us. "I was too busy this fall. The garden got away from me. It's better for me to bring it to you." It's still a barter as far as I'm concerned, but I'm learning that barter is less the exchange of one specific thing for another specific thing and something more profound and simple: a way of doing and being, a way of tasting the ordinary goodness that weaves its way through a broken world.

Today Greg is making sauerkraut and rainbow slaw, and for the freezer tomato soup base, braised cabbage, bags of chopped bell peppers, zucchini loaf. Today the kitchen is a little food factory. The season's harvest is unexpected and bountiful and we are grateful.

My Parsnip Harvest

Parsnips sounded quaint and rustically charming, like something out of *Peter Rabbit*. Yet I believe they are ordinary fare for Nova Scotians, or at least still held honourably in the collective Nova Scotian memory. Skipper speaks of them fondly. But I had never seen one that I knew of, much less eaten one. As I've written before, I am a refugee from an over-developed culture, and the whole idea of food coming from seeds planted in the earth was mind-bending for me.

But I read about parsnips somewhere, and they were described as an overlooked vegetable with a delicate taste. "I like them," Greg said last spring, when I consulted him on what to plant. It never occurred to me to wonder how he knew he liked them. Since as far as I knew he hadn't had any in the past twenty years or so. Greg has this mythical childhood well of knowledge that he can evoke whenever you try to push him. I bought a packet of seeds.

The first planting did not go well. But then, most of the first plantings of everything got washed away in a series of spring deluges. I planted the seeds again. And again. Somewhere along the way I read that parsnips are like that. The seeds themselves are sulky, easily offended, and often don't germinate, maybe just to spite themselves. You must keep replanting and replanting until they do. That was encouragement enough, a kind of affirmation that my personal experience was a common one. I did not feel so alone with my failed parsnip row, and after it finally took hold and began to grow its big dark leaves, I even went so far as to plant a second row.

By then I was actually falling in love with parsnips. I began to realize that they were good for the lazy gardener. Once the leaves have emerged from the ground all you need to do is wait. And you can pull them any time you like, the later the better. Frost only improves their taste. There's nothing urgent about the parsnip harvest. They are iffy and hard to please in the start-up phase, but once they take hold they are constant. I liked that.

And at the end I discovered one more good thing about parsnips. They are beneath the notice of deer and sheep. I guess it's because of their poisonous leaves, although when those two gangs broke into the garden they gobbled up the tomatoes and peppers, stems, leaves and all, which are also said to be poisonous. But after the garden was laid low the parsnips still stood, heroic in an overlooked kind of way.

So I have begun to harvest them. So far I have pulled up about a dozen, and there are another three dozen still in the ground. The first ones were a revelation: huge white things that had grown deep beneath the soil, all unbeknownst. Some were fancied-up with extraneous waving rootlettes that gave them a certain aura of zaniness, like they'd try anything once. Others were sober and long and thick and pale -- iconic parsnips, a fitting food in this province of fish and bread and tea, as Elizabeth Bishop calls Nova Scotia in her poem "The Moose".

Greg has found a recipe for parsnip patties in the old *Farm Journal Cookbook*, and I'm sure there is a parsnip and leek and potato soup in our future. We could call it Left Alone Soup, since those are the three vegetables in our garden that the deer and sheep ignored.

Lessons from Apples

We have over forty apple trees and they are very old. We think William Perry planted them in the late nineteenth century. I'm slowly identifying at least the types of trees and learning about apple characteristics in the process. I pore over pictures of old apples and swish their names around in my mind: Golden Russet, Alexander, Ashmead's Kernel, Cox's Orange Pippin, Bishop's Pippin, Gravenstein, Maiden's Blush, Rhode Island Greening, Early August, Transcendent Crab. There are hundreds of old apple varieties, and some of them have aliases, too. It isn't that easy to make a positive identification. But at least we are learning – in a general sense – what each tree is like, by paying attention to them and taking notes every fall. A tree might be biennial, filled with apples one year and empty the next. It could bear early or late. It could be a good eating apple or better for tarts, or cider. We learn a little more about this old orchard with each succeeding harvest.

One of the great lessons of the island is that the more closely you observe something the more beautiful it becomes. Most of these apples would not fare well in a market. They are small and oddly shaped and their colors are subtle rather than bright. But the more I looked at their peculiarities -- their russeting, blush, streaking, the little pin point dots called lenticels which can be green or white or bronze -- the more I recognized their beauty.

It wasn't until we had been on the island for well over a year that we first made cider. That fall we started picking apples in early October, and by the middle of the month Greg had assembled our new cider press. We were ready to go. We spent a dizzying few days trying to press and store sixty or seventy gallons of cider. We gave away lots of it fresh, froze as much as we could, and started the hard cider process with about twenty gallons. As usual, we barely knew what we were doing, but we were willing to learn from our mistakes, if only we could remember what they were.

Neither of us had ever been a particular fan of apple juice or the cider you could buy in the store. It was sweet and insipid. But now we have a new perspective. After our first pressing we held a two person tasting of the cider from each of trees, and discovered that the tastes were quite different -- except toward the end, when they all tasted pretty much the same and we couldn't touch another drop. We were more ambitious back then, thinking we would blend the ciders and name them. Now we just mix the juice as it comes pouring out of the cider press. The jugs go into the freezer, and later they make their way, one at a time, into the refrigerator. Then all year after that you open the refrigerator, pull out the jug, pour a glass, and drink the intense taste of hundred year old apple trees.

Visit to the Yellow Birch Tree

Along the main road, near the place where the osprey nest, is a stand of old yellow birch trees. The biggest of them sits apart. Its thick scarred roots spread out and sink down into a moss covered hillock that gives softly beneath your feet, so that you come near with care, as if approaching an ancient sacred place.

The trunk of this tree has been twisted by centuries of swirling wind and its bark is deeply creviced, almost black with age. A whole branch, itself as big as a mature tree, has grown far out from the main trunk and rests its weight on the ground, slowly undulating away in the direction of the cove.

The tree wears the calamities of age. Yet as hollow and ravaged and scarred as it is, it is deeply alive, dappled and pied with lichen and moss, home to innumerable insects and small burrowing creatures. It is thought to be the largest and oldest yellow birch tree in Nova Scotia. It doesn't matter whether this is true: the tree is a wonder just in itself.

Laundry

I do love the way laundry claims order out of chaos on such a manageable scale. When we arrived here way back in the summer of ought seven, the house had neither electricity nor plumbing. For a month or so I drew water by the pail full from an old stone-lined well, heated it on the Coleman camp stove, and washed our clothes under an ancient apple tree, by hand. There was a washboard in the house when we arrived, and I used that, too, and a galvanized tub. In my hazy memory of that summer, the sky was always blue and the sun bounced off the glittering harbour waters spread out before me as I stepped, awed, into a pre-industrial life.

But as much as I enjoyed washing the clothes that summer, I like our washing machine even better. It's quite a basic machine, and it uses lots more energy than the new-fangled ones do. So I wait until a sunny and windy day, like today, to wash the clothes. Of course those are the best days for drying laundry anyway, so everything hangs together: another small sign of order.

After years of throwing the clothes in the dryer, I take enormous pleasure in hanging them on the line. I love that the sun and the wind have their way with them. And I love drying the dishes with these fresh dish towels and sleeping on these fresh sheets.

Our clothes line is suspended between two of the old apple trees, and runs alone a stone wall, inside the back orchard. By this time of year the stone walls are probably filled with dozing creatures, undisturbed by flapping dish towels or thoughts of domestic order, just drifting off for their winter sleep.

Grape Harvest

It turned out that Elizabeth Hyde planted our grape vine, long ago: a Concord, maybe. After Elizabeth died the house and the land more or less went to sleep, but those vines continued to grow along the ground up where she had her big vegetable garden. Skipper, who always kept an eye on things, built a wooden fence around them to keep the sheep and deer from plundering them. So when we first arrived, the vines lay tangled and forlorn inside and over the remains of a weather-beaten wooden fence.

After our first year we took down that old fence and included the vines inside the new vegetable garden. Ambitiously, Greg built an arbour for the grapes. We pruned them and trained them, sort of. But there was only so much we could do besides tearing out the single huge trunk and starting over. Which I wasn't that interested in. The arbour was pretty enough in the garden's second summer, with its vines growing this way and that and its translucent leafy canopy. Last year we got maybe a cup of grapes, and Greg made one little jar of grape jelly. I figured we had built the arbour for the benefit of our bird friends, and I left it at that.

This year I paid no attention to the grape arbour. As summer went on some vines got too long and started hitting me in the face as I walked into the garden, so I whacked them off. But that was as far as any pruning went. Gradually, though, I started noticing that there were clusters of grapes forming here and there. Oh well, I thought, the birds will be happy this year. I did not get my hopes up. I barely looked at the arbour. After all, I had collards to consider, and chard, and beans. Important things. Quietly, behind my back, the grapes grew.

This past week was apple harvesting time around here. The big-time action was all in the apple trees, but in the middle of the week Greg mentioned that he thought the grapes were ready to harvest, too. So I picked the grapes, about four and a half gallons once I took them off their stems.

Though we should have been putting two and two together all along, the bounty of the grape arbour caught us off guard. I had thought that the birds would swoop in at the last and stage a gigantic avian grape-fest, and that whatever we got would be an afterthought, their leftovers. But now instead we had oh-so-much of a good thing, requiring immediate attention. The rushing torrent of apple momentum would have to wait.

Jam was what we aspired to, not merely jelly. Not something smooth and simple and jelly-like, but something dense, more complex. But it turns out that jam -- as opposed to jelly -- is complicated to make. There are many time-consuming steps. These are the ones I did: taking the grapes off the stems, then separating the pulp from the skin of each and every grape. So that you end up with a pot of pulp, which is called must, and a separate bowl of skins. As far as I know there is no machine for doing this, or at least not at our house.

After that I turned everything over to Greg. I can't even tell you how many steps came next, since I stayed out of the kitchen. There were many, many steps, involving rarely-used and mysterious equipment and supplies. All evening, until midnight, the kitchen was filled with the purple aroma of grapes and the reading out loud of snippets from various recipes pulled off the Internet, which sounded like nothing so much as the muttering of charms and spells.

This morning I came downstairs to discover magic jars of grape jam, more than I can count, a rich dark colour amidst the brightness of the apple harvest.

At the Mercy of the Wind

Our high-tech wind turbine and the solar tracker work together, and that's good. Because some days we have wind and no sun, and other days we have sun and no wind. On really glorious days we have both. That's when we turn on all sorts of energy-sucking rigs: the washing machine, the vacuum cleaner, the crock pot, the little hot water heater. We have a new dehydrator, for drying apples. But we can only use it on sunny and windy days, when our energy production is high. And we have a second freezer now, for freezing all that fresh apple cider -- about fifty gallons. It's an old freezer and even though it works well it adds to our energy load.

If we have a string of cloudy and windless days, the batteries that store all the energy lose their charge. Down, down, down they slide, while we turn off lights and computers. We do have a back-up for times when the batteries get too low: a ten thousand watt propane generator sits on a concrete pad behind the battery shed. The generator goes on automatically when the system calls for it. We don't let it run for very long though, since it uses up propane. We hear its motor kick on, even in the middle of the night, and one of us goes out to the shed and re-sets everything. By then the generator has kicked up the charge in the batteries at least enough to keep them going for a while.

A string of six propane tanks, strung together by copper gas lines, sits in the former outhouse, a shed next to the shed that houses the batteries and all the fancy blinking lights for the whole business. There's no measuring device for the propane tanks, an odd gap in all this technology. The only way you can tell how much propane is left in those tanks is to look for a line of condensation along the outside of the tanks. It should tell you where the level of your propane is. But you need to be looking for that condensation on a wet day. Because on a dry day you can't see it.

Yesterday we ran out of propane. But that was okay because Greg had an extra tank, which he attached to the end of the string of tanks, thus giving us a little lee-way until he could go into town to get the tanks re-filled. But then the stove ran out of propane too. The stove has been very much in use for blanching beans and chard et cetera, and canning grape jam and apple sauce et cetera. So then Greg took the one full tank back off the string of tanks in the shed and replaced the empty tank at the stove. So now, no propane back up for the generator until Saturday, when he can go into town. But he can certainly carry on with the apple tarts and apple jelly and apple chutney.

There is no sun expected here until Sunday, and today is Wednesday. According to the weather reports it'll be mostly rain between now and then. If the charge on the batteries goes too low we'll just watch everything go off. Then there will be no running water or flushing toilet or freezer keeping everything from the garden frozen or computers bringing us the world at our fingertips, or lights. For the next few days we are living at the mercy of the wind.

These are hardly dire conditions, though. After all, we do have a back-up back-up system: an outhouse, and oil lamps, and an old well we can drop a bucket into, and little rainy-day projects that don't require electricity, like re-gluing broken plates and organizing closets. We do have books.

Gathering Rosehips

The forager learns that an awkward path can lead toward gladness. To find wild raspberries you will clamber over fallen spruce trunks while their sharp spiky branches ward you away and the bees await to mount a final defense. To collect chanterelles you will squat or kneel along the roadside, or lie upon the earth in some forest glade, crawling on your belly beneath low spruce branches. To harvest cranberries you will creep through the bog, your rubber boots squishing as you pull each foot out of the mire, carefully, so as not to end up leaving your boot behind.

On the other hand, to gather rosehips you can just jump on the ATV and travel far and wide to reach the biggest of the wild rose bushes you have noticed from time to time. The bushes themselves are not hard to get to. Beginning this adventure is easy.

But once you are standing in front of a rosebush, you will need to consider. There are thorns. You will be able to avoid the obvious thorns, the big ones. But there are also tiny thorns too small to notice. Those you learn about more directly, by feeling them. You will pay a miniscule amount for your rosehips, only a drop or two of blood.

The best rosehips will always be beyond your reach -- way up high, or nestled deep within a crisscrossing of branches. Those are there only for you to look at and admire. The birds -- more adept at these kinds of things -- will gather them, not you. Later, the memory of collecting rosehips will remain with you, in your fingers, at the places where tiny thorns are embedded.

Each adventure in foraging has its own joy, its own brief intimacy with the island's secret places. But always there is the joy of colour. Raspberries glow like jewels -- amethysts, or rubies. The chanterelles are apricot gold that gleams fitfully among dark spruce needles and green moss and earth. Cranberries are pink mottled with pale yellow, then damson or grape and slowly emerging crimson. Rosehips do not gleam or glow. Instead they shine as bright as autumn fire.

Deer Season

This evening the deer family is in the lower orchard. They aren't easy to see, since they are the colour of the wet bark of old apple trees, or of rain-darkened boulders. They blend in. I can see them, though, because their movement attracts my eye. In this I think my eye has become more discerning during the past two and half years. I notice movement better now, and maybe shape: the patterned flicker of grass where a snake is passing; the cupped curve of a nest. My eyesight is terrible, but experience has begun to compensate. I have learned that if I notice something I ought to pay attention. Maybe that's the whole difference, right there, between now and then.

The deer remain mysterious, but they have begun to come into focus for us. One of the books that came with the house was *The World of the White-tailed Deer*, by Leonard Lee Rue III (Philadelphia: Lippincott, 1962.) The book belonged to Howard T. Walden 2nd, who was Elizabeth Hyde's father and a well-respected nature writer, especially about fly fishing. His penciled under linings and marginal notes are a conversation between the reader and the writer. Maybe, too, they are notes on an inner dialogue inspired by his reading the book and remembering the deer he has seen in his life. It's like catching a few words from a distant thought, or like the hint of a deer as it leaps away, some foggy evening sixty or seventy years ago.

Rue tells me that deer stay in a three-generation matriarchal family composed in its simplest form of the older doe, the younger doe and the younger doe's offspring. He also says that they inhabit a one-square mile area for their entire lives, and move outside that area only in extreme conditions. That explains why, all fall, we have only seen this one family, and another solitary deer as well. There are other deer on the island, other families, but they inhabit other places.

The hunters were here only for the first couple of weeks of deer season. After that, they turn their attention back to the final touches of getting ready for lobster season, and the island grows quiet again. We call them the hunters, but really they are our same friends who have camps on the island and come over now and then during the summer. Their interest in the deer gives them an intimate connection to the island. Once a year they cut deep into the forest where nobody else ever goes, and build their secret places, and watch and wait. Because they take the time and because they pay attention they see more than the rest of us, I think.

Some of their wives tell them, "Fine, go off to McNutt's and hunt. Just don't kill anything." They do, though, and I think it's probably a good thing. There's not much killing of deer that takes place, but what does probably helps the herd as a whole. If there are too many deer on the island they will starve over the winter. Already the hunters are concerned about what they saw during this hunting season: deer smaller and thinner than they have seen in years past. It makes sense. This summer was not abundant for growing things. For a few weeks the hunters host the deer at lavish feasts of apples and carrots. But even so, the deer may be going into the winter with little reserve.

Musselling

Mussel season begins about now, so I went along the shore to look for some. In past years mussels have come to us like grace: unexpected, unmerited, a bucket brimful and running over. But we would like to learn the secret ways of mussels for ourselves. When I have asked where they are to be found, the answer is, "Oh, on some rocks along the shore." I've been told that they are easy to find. This is not my experience, yet. But I imagine that after I have found the mussels, then they will be easy to find.

Mussel hunting may be best accomplished in a little boat, floating quietly and closely toward the big rocks that sit half exposed, half submerged in the cove's tide. Since my rowboat is now up on dry land, I searched by walking along the shore at low tide, sometimes lifting up the shiny black strands of seaweed that festoon the rocks, peering beneath for sight of shiny black mussels clinging in colonies to the rock's surface.

The ebbing tide reveals abundant fields of rockweed. Underwater, when the tide is higher, the plants are in their element and they wave about gracefully, their branches floating on tiny balloons of air, their stems firmly attached to the shore's rocks. They are in their element at low tide, too, though their element has changed. Now they lie along the rocks, fully exposed to air and sunlight. They thrive in this constant process of ebb and flow.

Since I am hunting mussels at low tide I walk out on rockweed to reach the bigger rocks. They are slick masses that obscure the rocks, which are themselves unstable, having been thrown here by storm and waves, and being just as likely to roll away again: another constantly changing element. I walk slowly, a balancing act. Really, no matter how well you study the situation, there is too much that is unknown, and no telling what will happen until you take the next step. It's probably foolish of me to be walking here.

The mink may think as much. He pops his head up and stares at me, then flattens himself against his home rock, mink coat blending perfectly with his eelgrass cover. I watch him for a while. I would like to make my peace with him and his kin. I have held it against them that they are not native to the island. But neither are the sheep, or the deer, or us, for that matter. He is a part of something that is always changing. I wish the mink would confine themselves to the shore and not go hunting around our house and along the lower road for snakes and rabbits. But maybe they were especially hungry this summer. Maybe the fish didn't come into the cove as plentifully as in years past. Anyway, the mink belong to the island's reality as much as I do.

I did find something we had been hunting for: the boundary rock marked with Jonathan Perry's initials. It stands at the southwest corner of Jonathan's original plot, the one he bought from the first lighthouse keeper and later divided between his two sons. On the Grant Map of 1784 this is part of Lot Number One, granted to Moses Pitcher, glazier, one of thousands of American colonists who chose loyalty to the British during the American Revolution. In some ways the Loyalists were flotsam and jetsam along the rocky shores of Empire. Some of them took root here. Most -- including Moses Pitcher -- rolled out again on the ebb tide. For now his property belongs to us by deed, and to the mink by squat, and to the mussels whether I can find them or not.

Cranberry Walkabout

On the south side of the island, hoping for cranberries, I picked up the ghostly track of an ATV. Maybe it was our own from this time last year. I doubt if anyone has come there since. I followed it, walking through a low scrum of bayberry and juniper and cotton grass and dried fern, around stands of spruce and up a gentle crest. Surrounded by the forest and the sea and hidden in a low place, the bog becomes visible only when you are upon it. Like so much on the island, if you don't know where to look you will only discover it by accident. And if, having found it, you fail to take sufficient note of where you are, you may not find it again.

Once I was in the bog I tiptoed about in my rubber boots, a curious giantess, and bent down and squatted so I could peer closely at this world. Everywhere I looked I saw the basal leaves of the pitcher plant, plump veined red teacups. Each one now held a thimble-full of some dark shining brew. The pitcher plant seems to have had a very good year in this bog. I might have come upon the last touches for an end-of-season tea-party about to be tossed by the local fairies for a few invited flies. While I admired the cunning place-settings, the guests, abuzz, were at home donning their iridescent wings and polishing their heads.

Even though it is a small enough place -- maybe four or five acres altogether -- and even though you can see all the way across it no matter where you are standing, still, it's easy to lose your way in this bog. Somehow you are never quite where you had thought you were. You look up from peering into its watery pathways and glinty pools and rumpled velvet moss to find yourself somewhere else entirely. How did I get over here when I was just over there, you wonder. I think there may be some shape-shifting that befalls the bog visitor, which can be disconcerting unless you begin to go with it.

It is easy to forget that, like a reasonable person, I have come here for a reason. I remember from last year's search that to see these cranberries I will need to adjust my expectations. I won't be looking for the colour we call cranberry red. Instead, I'm after a glimpse of dull purplish bloom only a few shades darker than the pitcher plant's teacups. I remember Peter's rule for seeing whales in the summer. "Go up to the lighthouse four or five times in

July," he said, "and look out to sea, and I guarantee you, if you do that four or five times, on one of those trips you'll see a whale."

Peter's rule applies to cranberries too (and maybe to other things as well). I spied one, then another, then another, until I had gathered a handful in my cupped palm. If I bent down to look four or five times, on one of those times I'd begin to find them lying quietly about here and there, attached to a delicate green thread, a dark jewel set on a bracelet of tiny green leaves, bog treasure.

It's All about Wood, Continued

Our relationship to firewood has continued to evolve since we first arrived in Nova Scotia. Back then, our most recent experience with actual fire -- as opposed to heat coming out of radiators --was a gas log fireplace. Which was pretty nice, really, with its remote control and all. Quite cozy. And nothing but icing on the cake, since back then the real heat was supplied by some mysterious furnace in the basement that we hardly ever even gave a thought to, even when we probably should have.

Here, we saw right away that by the end of April most people already had huge wide orderly walls of next winter's wood sitting in their yards, cords and cords of it, split and stacked and drying. It was a little intimidating to imagine the amount of labour involved in this one housekeeping item. But it was exciting, too. We had wanted to deal with life on a more elementary level. What could be more elementary than providing our own heat from start to finish instead of writing a monthly cheque to the anonymous purveyors of oil or gas or electricity?

As we observed our new environment more closely, we saw that many people kept their wood in an actual extra old house or shed. This is not the sort of thing you notice right away, stacked firewood peering out of the windows of old buildings. Instead it's a telling detail that reveals itself in due time, when you are ready to see it.

The back room of this very house was an attached wood shed before it became a guest room in the 1960s. Keeping the firewood dry and getting to it easily was not a problem for the families that lived in this house before us. But it was for us, at least until now.

Now Greg has finished building our covered wood shed. He used spruce poles for the uprights and recycled local lumber for the rest. He planned it with a big overhang in front to cut down on the effect of weather that blows in from the southwest, as it mostly does. And also so I will have cover while I'm getting wood off the pile.

This is a huge improvement over our first and second winters, when I tried to keep the woodpile dry with big pieces of heavy plastic sheeting, secured against the wind by random logs and stones. It worked okay except when it didn't, and during those first awkward years our neighbours maintained a charitable, tactful silence that allowed us to learn from our own experience.

The Great Mandala

Each autumn as the weather turns cold again, the deer mice come back into the innards of the house. They arrive through their secret passages, the ones that we will never close up, no matter how alert or ingenious or dedicated we are. And from there, their safe places, at night, while we are asleep upstairs, they enter the kitchen. Where we have set out mouse traps, baited with cheese. Thus begins the sad but inevitable dance: dance of cheese or death.

We do not hate the mice. They are beautiful and charming animals. If only they didn't want to live inside the house, but of course they do want to live here in this warmly crumby place. And there's no co-existing, no compromise that would suit both parties. So, with regret, we kill them off, one by one. And with determination or hopefulness or filial piety, their children and their grandchildren keep coming back to this fabled paradise, the place they hold dear in their collective memory, our kitchen.

A couple of years ago, in the dregs of winter, when there's hardly anything left out there to eat, we began an understanding with the ravens. It was they who thought of it first, swooping closer to the house than we'd ever seen them do before, stalking and preening around in the side yard. Before, they had mostly perched in the spruce trees south of the house, or in the lower orchard apple trees, or flapped in threes and sevens into the dead forest along the shore where the owl lives. They are birds of great size and dignity, and we were surprised to see them coming so close.

On the nights when we ate meat --lamb or venison or mutton, all from the island --we were then in the habit of putting the bones and scraps outside on a bench until the next day, when I would carry them down to the wharf and drop them into the water, for the gulls. One morning Greg saw a raven fly up off the bench. He had torn open the plastic bag and taken the scraps. Then we began to lay the left-overs on the cement platform of the solar tracker: an offering to the ravens. And soon we added the morning's mouse corpse to the collection. The ravens took it all, lifting into flight with their claws firmly holding these gifts.

Season of Good Cheer

There's a quality of good cheer about deer hunting season on the island. The "hunters" are the same people as our neighbours, only for a couple of weeks they dress differently. As far as I can tell they have customary hunting rights over the whole island, which means that whoever I see riding by on an ATV belongs with one of our neighbours. It's usually one of their fishing mates and some younger relatives who are gradually learning the ways of hunting under more experienced eyes. So, since it's pretty much the same people year after year, they take a great deal of interest in how the deer population is doing. I would say they know more about the habits of the island's deer than anyone else. They are, really, students of the deer.

I'm glad to see them every fall because it's my chance to ask questions and learn something about the mysterious ways of deer. I try not to ask too much. I don't want to seem like I'm prying. So I limit myself to a question or two per year. This year I learned that the bucks usually stay deep in the woods while the does and fawns wander about more. That's why we see does and fawns around the house and sometimes on the road, but hardly ever do we see bucks. Just because we don't see them doesn't mean they aren't there.

The bucks become less cautious, though, as rutting season strikes them. I learned from the hunters this week that it's the onset of cold weather that triggers the bucks' desire to mate and lures them out of their hiding places. Deer season began officially last Friday, but it only started to get cold a couple of days ago. They said something about the phases of the moon too, but I didn't understand that part. I'll wait until next year to find out more about that.

I like the sound of their ATVs going up and down the road, heading toward their blinds deep in the woods or to another camp, then back again. Each year in late October they clear out their old ATV paths into the interior. Their paths do us good, since we can walk along them at other times of the year and explore an otherwise impenetrable landscape of forest and bog.

I don't think of hunting season as a tragedy for the deer. Most of the deer who gather around the piles of imported carrots and apples to help themselves are does and fawns and under-sized bucks, and can't be shot. Maybe the carrots and apples they are eating now will add to the reserves they need to get through the winter. And if the hunters decide the herd seems too small and the bucks too few, they will just agree among themselves not to shoot any. Since they have been hunting here for years, they take the long view. Sometimes I think they are more interested in watching the deer than anything else. But they are truly happy when one of their group bags one.

They enjoy being out here for a few days anyway. The young fellas are learning the ways of the woods. The old fellas are getting away from the mainland and enjoying a break between the end of fishing and the start of the lobster season in a few weeks, when they'll be hunting beneath the deep, cold North Atlantic waters.

Epilogue

It was humbling to come home again after a two-month absence. We had never been away from the island for more than a week, before, and that only once. Now we returned to a freshly fallen foot or so of snow. After we docked we trudged through it up the hill to the house, lugging only a few grocery bags. The rest of the stuff would have to wait at the boat. We were relieved to find that the freezer, holding several months' worth of food, was still working. Before we left we had turned off the rest of the electricity and drained the pipes. It only took a little while to restore the house, now dormant for two months, to working order. I had imagined that it would take a long time to warm the living room, but by supper time it was cozy again.

The next day Skipper came by, saying that it was the first time he'd visited the island since we left. So nobody at all had been here while we were away. As soon as our boat steamed away from the dock in mid December, the old silence enveloped everything again until we returned.

I think a kind of enchantment falls upon McNutt's Island when its people go away. Maybe it has been like this since the beginning of time. I suspect that those who have claimed it as home over the centuries have known that in truth we are at most making a visit here. This is a place that nobody can possess, where nobody leaves much of a mark. It belongs instead to wave and wind and spruce and rock and gull. Left alone, it only takes a minute or two before the island sloughs off any memory of its human inhabitants and slips again into a deep quiet.

And now it receives us back with the indifference of a small primal wilderness. You may stay, the island seems to tell us, as long as you know your place.

Made in the USA
San Bernardino, CA
18 August 2014